T0147184

Feasting
AT
WISDOM'S
TABLE

A STUDY IN PROVERBS
VOLUME 1

JOSEPH W. COWAN

WESTBOW
PRESS®
A DIVISION OF THOMAS NELSON
& ZONDERVAN

WestBow Press books may be ordered through booksellers or by contacting:

WestBow Press
A Division of Thomas Nelson & Zondervan
1663 Liberty Drive
Bloomington, IN 47403
www.westbowpress.com
844-714-3454

Scripture quotations taken from the (NASB®) New American Standard Bible®, Copyright © 1960, 1971, 1977, 1995, 2020 by The Lockman Foundation. Used by permission. All rights reserved. www.lockman.org

ISBN: 978-1-6642-4986-8 (sc)
ISBN: 978-1-6642-4987-5 (hc)
ISBN: 978-1-6642-4985-1 (e)

Library of Congress Control Number: 2021923219

Print information available on the last page.

WestBow Press rev. date: 11/22/2021

CONTENTS

Before the decree takes effect—
The day passes like the chaff—
Before the burning anger of the LORD comes upon you,
Before the day of the Lord's anger comes upon you.
Seek the LORD,
All you humble of the earth,
Who have carried out His ordinances;
Seek righteousness, seek humility.
Perhaps you will be hidden in the day of the LORD's anger.

Zephaniah 2:2–3

FOREWORD

I have known Joe Cowan for over thirty years and he has always used the book of Proverbs in his everyday conversations. Whether reciting word for word or paraphrasing, this timeless treasure of wisdom has always been on his lips.

Joe is a man of serious thought and deep conviction. His commentary/study on the book of Proverbs is a great reflection of his commitment to pragmatic truth.

Joe's life has been focused on the church's great mandate of making disciples. This commentary/study is going to be a great help in fulfilling the Lord's great commission. Joe has articulated the truths of these Proverbs and highlighted the many spiritual nuggets that are found in them.

I am excited to take men through this commentary and to also use it in small group Bible studies. The questions after each chapter naturally lead to rich dialogue and self-examining inspections. On a personal note this will be a great addition in my personal devotions as I go before the throne of grace.

> "How blessed is the man who finds wisdom And the man who gains understanding. For her profit is better than the profit of silver And her gain better than fine gold." (Proverbs 3:13–14 NASB® 1995)

Sam Johnson
Chaplain for the San Antonio Spurs

PREFACE

I have been in over 60 US cities from the west coast to the east coast, from north to the south. The American people are a great people, our country is a great land.

Yet there are things that have gone wrong in our land that only an authentic relationship with God can change. Our land has become so secularized. Few people are giving God reverence in their personal lives. Respect towards one another suffers in our public interactions. The United States of America is quite divided.

Where are we heading as a nation? Healing (not medical but spiritual healing) for our hearts, families, cities, states and country is in view. Our founding fathers could not establish this nation apart from the Lord. We cannot keep it without the Lord. God is infinitely greater than our problems. Our nation can be healed. Much depends on people's response to God. There is still hope. A study such as this can help us examine our lives and our relationship with God.

There is rebuilding to do. Those that do it must do it with reliance on the guidance of Divine Providence. It begins in each one's own heart. The Lord God Almighty is the One who ultimately rules, and to Him we must all—great or small, rich or poor, leaders and non-leaders, members of all ethnic groups, creeds, religions and no religions—we must all give account to God as to how we have lived.

This study is structured to be used either as an individual study, or in a group setting. At the beginning of each chapter you are encouraged to read the passage. The theme of the teaching in each chapter is drawn from a single verse in the passage, and is developed by supporting applications drawn from related principles in selected scriptures of the same passage. At the end of each lesson you will find a deductive study in the form of a chart. These are helpful to get a perspective of the whole chapter as to how the verses can be related to each other. There are two deductive charts after the table of contents as well. One gives the overall picture of the entire book of Proverbs the other focuses on the first fifteen chapters. Also, you will find questions for further study at the end of each chapter. They are written in an attempt to provoke deep thought. Try to take time to think through the questions. It will be beneficial to you. There is an *Appendix of Analytical Charts* starting with chapter 10. These are for the person who wants to do inductive studies on the individual verses of each passage. They follow the basic format of scripture, observations, applications and cross references.

The purpose of this study is to aid believers to draw nearer to God. We are taught that wisdom's beginning is in the fear of the Lord, and that leads to a personal, experiential and intimate relationship with the One who created the universe and all that is in it. (Proverbs 9:10)

May the Lord grant that through this study of Proverbs, that each one who applies those things found in the book of Proverbs, will grow in the reverence for God and will gain the understanding and encouragement to walk in the higher path of righteousness and turn away from the things that destroy.

Joseph W Cowan
July 4, 2021

ACKNOWLEDGMENTS

It is always appropriate to make known to people those whose influence contributed to the completion of a work such as this. So I am dedicating some space for this very purpose.

Apart from the Lord, I never would have attempted to do this study, but the Lord is the One who has saved my life from the folly in my own heart. He used people and His word (especially the book of Proverbs) to do it.

He has always brought people around me who loved Him and loved me enough to tell me the truth. When I remember some of those people, I am moved in the depths of my heart with such gratitude because of the powerful impact upon my life which changed the course of my life. So I thank God who is my Beloved Daddy in heaven. He is always there in the midst of our daily lives. He actively and sovereignly superintends our very steps and guides us into His ways which are so much higher than our ways.

He used the Bowens to invite me to a revival meeting in Sumter, South Carolina where I was born from above. He used Pastor Stanley Bach in Oklahoma City to encourage me during my high school days. He used George Romer, a fellow soldier and mature believer, in a very special way to mentor me at a crucial time in my life when I was stationed at Ft Hood, TX. He used Brother Chisolm and Brother Shoemaker who ran the servicemen's center in Killeen, TX. He used a man named Joe Stone and about 17 other bearded men carrying Bibles and quoting the scriptures and living a disciplined and dedicated life as extraordinary examples that I shall never forget. And I am so grateful for each one of them for God used them, every one of them, mightily in my life.

There was Tim Bell who used to meet a handful of us soldiers to pray, early on Monday mornings. Tim used Proverbs as a guide for our praying.

Then I found myself at IHOP on the weekends for a weekly Bible study in San Antonio, TX where we went through Proverbs (the very first time for me). I saved those studies, and later developed them by adding to them. God used Proverbs several times to steer me away from doing evil, and thus preserved my life.

Later, in Oceanside, CA, God used Warren and Peggy Hume who ran a servicemen's center there, and Peggy had a tremendous influence upon my thinking.

Then Wayne Thrasher, President of Texas Bible College in San Antonio, who helped transform the way I studied the Bible in the early 1990's .

The Lord used all these, and godly men like Brother Art Stacer, a retired Air Force Sergeant and faithful prayer warrior, who remains such a precious brother in my life.

But it was my pastors, Sam Johnson and Mike Pratt who urged me to write. Without their urging when they did, I don't know if I would have ever written this study, so I say, "Thank you, my dear brothers, for speaking to me.

But the most important one of all is Maire Archbold-Cowan, my wife. Without your encouragement, Honey, I would have given up on this project. I so appreciate your prayers, encouragement and you taking the time to edit the manuscript in the midst of your battles that you face daily. You're special and I honor you. Thank you so much.

To My Beloved Children

The Fear of the Lord:
A Call to Know and Understand the Holy One

1:1-2:22	The Fear Of The Lord And The Beginning Of Wisdom	The Introduction to the Book of Proverbs	The Fear of the Lord: A Call to Know and Understand the Holy One
3:1-4:27	The Basic Teachings Of Wisdom		
5:1-7:27	Things That Divide, Deceive and Destroy		
8:1-9:18	The Crossroads Of Wisdom OR Folly		
10:1-22:16	The Proverbs Of Solomon	A Great Feast of Wisdom and Understanding	
22:17-24:22	The Sayings Of The Wise		
25:1-29:27	Solomon's Proverbs Collected by Hezekiah's Men		
30:1-33	The Words Of Agur		
31:1-31	The Words Of King Lemuel		

THE BOOK PROVERBS CHAPTERS 1–15

1:1-33	Motivations For Wisdom	The Fear of the LORD and the Beginning of Wisdom	The Introduction to the Book of Proverbs
2:1-22	How To Find Wisdom, Knowledge And Understanding		
3:1-35	The Pillars Of Wisdom	The Basic Teaching of Wisdom	
4:1-27	The Teaching Of A Godly Father		
5:1-23	The Sobering Dangers Of Adultery	Things that Divide, Deceive and Destroy	
6:1-35	Some Dangerous Pitfalls		
7:1-27	The Naive Lad And The Adulteress		
8:1-21	Wisdom's Universal Call	The Crossroads of Wisdom or Folly	
8:22-31	Wisdom's Heritage		
8:32-36	Traits Of Those Who Love Wisdom		
9:1-12	Wisdom Reaches Out		
9:13-18	Folly Advertises		
10:1-32	Why One Should Desire Righteousness	The Proverbs of Solomon	A Great Feast of Wisdom and Understanding
11:1-31	The Characteristics Of The Righteous		
12:1-28	Counseling—A Painstaking Labor Of Love		
13:1-25	True Prosperity		
14:1-35	The Greatest Wisdom In This Life		
15:1-33	Disposition And The Tongue		

THE
INTRODUCTION
TO THE BOOK
OF PROVERBS

"To receive instruction in wise behavior, righteousness, justice and equity;" (Proverbs 1:3)

MOTIVATIONS FOR WISDOM

Read Proverbs 1:1–33.

Solomon, the son of David, king of Israel, opens his introduction to Proverbs by stating his purpose in writing them. These also become our motivations for studying this collection of wise sayings.

Now the scriptures say,

> "And God said to him, 'Because you have asked this thing and have not asked for yourself long life, nor have asked riches for yourself, nor have you asked for the life of your enemies, but have asked for yourself discernment to understand justice, behold, I have done according to your words. Behold, I have given you a wise and discerning heart, so that there has been no one like you before you, nor shall one like you arise after you. And I have also given you what you have not asked, both riches and honor, so that there will not be any among the kings like you all your days. And if you walk in My ways, keeping My statutes and commandments, as your father David walked, then I will prolong your days.' Then Solomon awoke, and behold, it was a dream." (1 Kings 3:11–15)

The biblical account of God coming to Solomon in a dream at the beginning of his reign in Israel and granting his request for "an understanding heart to judge Thy people to discern between good and evil" (1 Kings 3:9) is an extraordinary interaction recorded for us between the Lord and Solomon. It illustrates three marvelous things that we would do well to remember.

1. God is gracious. He took the initiative to come to Solomon and showed him unmerited favor.
2. God is the source of wisdom, understanding, discernment, and justice.
3. God gave wisdom to Solomon. This is what qualifies Solomon to speak these Proverbs. And this is a primary reason we need to take them to heart in a day when there seems to be a short supply of wisdom, understanding, discernment, and justice.

So Solomon gives his reasons for writing this book, saying first of all, "To know wisdom and instruction" (Proverbs 1:2).

What is wisdom? In one dictionary, we find this definition:

"The right use or exercise of knowledge; the choice of laudable ends, and of the best means to accomplish them. This is wisdom in act, effect, or practice."[1]

Proverbs are all about wisdom, which means one knows how to put knowledge into practice.

Secondly, Solomon tells us that we will:

"discern the sayings of understanding" (Proverbs 1:2).

Discernment is:

"the power or faculty of the mind, by which it distinguishes one thing from another, as truth from falsehood, virtue from vice; acuteness of judgment; power of perceiving differences of things or ideas, and their relations and tendencies."[2]

---

[1] Noah Webster, LLD, *An American Dictionary of the English Language* (S. Converse: New York, 1828, republished in facsimile edition by Foundation for American Christian Education: San Francisco, 1985).
[2] Ibid.

Consequently, reading through Proverbs, one finds that there is often a contrast or comparison between two things in order that one might be able either to distinguish the difference between the two or see the similarity that is common to the two.

Proverbs are all about enabling our minds to distinguish right from wrong, truth from error, and wisdom from folly.

The third purpose put forward by Solomon is:

> "To receive instruction in wise behavior, righteousness, justice and equity" (Proverbs 1:3)

Instruction is:

> "the act of teaching or informing the understanding in that of which it was before ignorant."[3]

Proverbs are all about giving us information with respect to wise behavior so that we may not remain ignorant—especially concerning righteousness, justice, and equity.

Finally, Solomon tells us that he intends for the proverbs "to give prudence to the naïve and to the youth knowledge and discretion" (Proverbs 1:4).

Discretion is:

> "that discernment which enables a person to judge critically of what is correct and proper, united with caution."[4]

It is especially important to the youth to have knowledge and discretion. Therefore, they should learn Proverbs so that they can carefully govern their conduct through the critical judgment of what is correct and proper.

Now let's look briefly at the results of hearing and understanding the Proverbs. Solomon says that the "wise man will hear and increase in learning" (Proverbs 1:5).

This word "hear" is more than just hearing audibly but "to attend; to listen; to obey."[5] In doing so with the Proverbs, you will receive an

---

[3] Ibid.
[4] Ibid.
[5] Ibid.

education such that your understanding is expanded and your learning is increased.

Proverbs are about expanding one's understanding and increasing one's learning with respect to the things of greatest value in this life.

Not only will your learning increase, but it says:

> "a man of understanding will acquire wise counsel" (Proverbs 1:5).

This means that a person will find guidance for important decisions in his or her life. Also this person will be able to counsel others who cross his or her path concerning important decisions they are facing as well.

It is essential to note that the wisdom of which Solomon writes is not inherent within the person but must be acquired.

Nor is it the natural wisdom of the world but the wisdom that originates with God. James in the New Testament speaks of both types of wisdom. He says:

> "But the wisdom from above is first pure, then peaceable, gentle, reasonable, full of mercy and good fruits, unwavering, without hypocrisy. And the seed whose fruit is righteousness is sown in peace by those who make peace." (James 3:17–18).

This is a beautiful description of wisdom coming from God. There is a secret to acquiring wisdom. What is it? It is:

> "the fear of the LORD" (Proverbs 1:7).

Solomon declares to all of us where it begins. Wisdom begins with God. Wisdom delivers us from our own folly locked within our hearts. And the results of wisdom bring God glory. The New Testament goes so far as to say:

> "Christ Jesus, who became to us wisdom from God" (1 Corinthians 1:30).

It could be said that if one has Christ dwelling in him or her, then that is wisdom. When He comes into a person's life, a union takes place between that person's spirit and the Holy Spirit, causing that person's spirit to come alive to God through faith in Christ. This is the essence of what it means to experience spiritual birth.

However, believing in Jesus Christ our Lord is not equal to the fear of the LORD. It is quite possible for a believer to have been born into God's family through faith in Jesus Christ yet not fear the LORD at all.

The fear of the LORD is most commonly thought of as reverence, or respect, toward God in one's behavior. The result would lead a person to turn away from evil.

Consider the following scriptures:

- Proverbs 8:13 says, "The fear of the LORD is to hate evil; pride and arrogance and the evil way, and the perverted mouth, I hate."
- Job 28:28 says, "And to man He said, 'Behold, the fear of the LORD, that is wisdom; And to depart from evil is understanding.'"
- In Ecclesiastes 12:13, Solomon says, "The conclusion, when all has been heard, is: fear God and keep His commandments, because this applies to every person."

We learn from the above-quoted scriptures that within the scope of reverence, and respect, toward God is the idea of hating evil. But hating evil alone does not show reverence toward God. Sometimes, we find ourselves doing the things that we hate (Romans 7:14–20). There must be a conscious departure from those things we no longer wish to do. However, if I turn away from something, I must turn toward something. I must do His commandments.

But what commandments must I do? I believe the apostle John summed it up simply for us so that we can grab hold of it. He says:

> "And this is His commandment, that we believe in the name of His Son Jesus Christ, and love one another, just as He commanded us" (1 John 3:23).

It is on the point of loving one another that we as believers often stumble.

And again, John says to born-again believers,

"Do not love the world, nor the things in the world. If anyone loves the world, the love of the Father is not in him. For all that is in the world, the lust of the flesh and the lust of the eyes and the boastful pride of life, is not from the Father, but is from the world."(1 John 2:15–16).

So if I believe in Jesus Christ but love the things in the world, I am still a believer, but I am not showing reverential respect toward God; I am not fearing God. I could say that I am acting foolishly. I am not keeping the greatest commandment, which is:

"And you shall love the Lord your God with all your heart and with all your soul and with all your might" (Deuteronomy 6:5).

This is important to understand. When Proverbs speaks of the righteous and the wicked, the wise and the fool, it is not necessarily talking about believers versus unbelievers, for a believer can do wickedly and a believer can become a fool.

The evil one, through the flesh, the world, or a direct assault:

- tries to entice us by a false promise (Proverbs 1:10–14).
- tries to deceive us through a sense of false security (verses 1:15–17).
- tries to lure us with something of temporal value (verses 1:13–14).

But wisdom cannot help those who do not choose to fear the LORD (verses 1:24–31).

Therefore, we end this chapter with a warning and a promise.

"For the waywardness of the
naïve shall kill them,
And the complacency of fools
shall destroy them.
But he who listens to me (wisdom) shall
live securely,
and shall be at ease from the dread of evil." (Proverbs 1:32–33)

Come, let us draw near to listen, to listen to wisdom from the Lord.

CHAPTER 1: WHY SHOULD ONE STUDY PROVERBS?

Motivations for Wisdom	**Introduction to the Book of Proverbs**	**The Purpose of Proverbs**	The title and author of the book	1.1
			To know wisdom and instruction to discern the sayings of understanding	1.2
			To receive instruction in wise behavior, righteousness, justice and equity	1.3
			To give prudence to the naïve, and knowledge and discretion to the youth	1.4
		The Results of Proverbs	A wise man will hear and increase in learning.	1.5a
			A man of understanding will acquire wise counsel.	1.5b
	The Great Importance of the Fear of the LORD	**The Secret of Proverbs**	The key to understanding a proverb —the fear of the Lord is the beginning of wisdom.	1.6, 7
			The instructions of the parents —it's important to listen to them.	1.8, 9
		The Law of The Harvest	The enticement —a false promise	1.10-14
			The deception —a false security	1.15-17
			The actual payoff —it costs you your life	1.18, 19
		The Availability of Wisdom	Wisdom reaches out in the midst of life.	1.20, 21
			Wisdom offers instruction to those who need it.	1.22, 23
			Wisdom cannot help those who do not choose the fear of the Lord.	1.24-31
			The certain expectation of the fool, and the promise for the wise.	1.32, 33

QUESTIONS FOR FURTHER STUDY

1. Proverbs 1:7 says, "The fear of the LORD is the beginning of knowledge; fools despise wisdom and instruction." Since the fear of the LORD is the beginning of knowledge, what is implied about the fool who hates wisdom and instruction?

2. Since the fear of the LORD is the beginning of knowledge, what must be true about the one who fears the LORD concerning his or her attitude toward instruction?

3. Psalm 111:10 says, "The fear of the LORD is the beginning of wisdom; a good understanding have all those who do His commandments." Both wisdom and knowledge are said to begin with the fear of the LORD. What is the difference between wisdom and knowledge?

4. James 3:13 says, "Who among you is wise and understanding? Let him show by his good behavior his deeds in the gentleness of wisdom." What does this tell us about how to express wisdom in our lives? What insight do you gain about wisdom from the focus of James? Considering Prov 1:7, what general principle must be true if I am to show anything in the gentleness of wisdom? What must I do first?

5. Consider James 3:14-18. What is the difference between earthly wisdom and the wisdom from above?

"For the LORD gives wisdom; from His mouth come knowledge and understanding." (Proverbs 2:6)

THREE CONDITIONS OF LEARNING SPIRITUAL TRUTH

Read Proverbs 2:1—22.

In 1Peter 2:2, there is an exhortation to grow up:

"Like newborn babies, long for the pure milk of the word, so
that by it you may grow in respect to salvation"(1Peter 2:2).

It is clear that a baby must have nourishment to grow physically. The
Bible tells us that this principle holds true if I am to grow in the knowledge
and understanding of spiritual life. I must have a steady diet of the word
of God.

This chapter begins by setting forth conditions, stipulating what must
happen to gain insight into the things of God.

The first condition to gain wisdom is an *attitude of teachability*. This
is implied in Proverbs 1:7 which reads,

"The fear of the LORD is the beginning of knowledge;
Fools despise wisdom and instruction."

One must be prepared to receive instruction. Solomon said to his son,

"My son, if you will receive my words…"(Proverbs 2:1).

God desires that His children would listen to Him as well.

If we are to make progress in studying Proverbs, we must come with an attitude that we are ready to learn. If we are not careful, we could close our mind to receiving something that we really need and not hear someone who really cares through an unteachable spirit.

According to the second verse, we receive the words of wisdom by making our "ear attentive" to those words and by applying our heart "to understanding" them. We always need to listen, if perhaps God may grant us to have some depth of understanding into what we have yet to come. It is essential to our healing to allow the barriers to be broken down so that learning and growth may take place.

Not only is one to be teachable, if he or she is to acquire wisdom, but there must be an appeal to God Himself. Thus we have the second condition of *earnest prayer.*

Proverbs 2:3 says, "If you *cry* for discernment."

The word cry comes from the Hebrew word transliterated *Quârâ* and means to "call out to."[6] Then the next phrase says,

"Lift your voice for understanding." (verse 2:3)

This is no passive praying going on here but rather one gets a sense of a person intensely and loudly calling out to God for much needed insight.

This is not to say that if someone asks silently for wisdom (at a moment in which it is needed) that God will not give it. On the contrary, in some cases a person needs to come up with an on the spot answer and a silent, urgent prayer within one's spirit is always answered with matchless wisdom.

But Proverbs 2:3 is emphasizing that this prayer for discernment and for understanding is quite audible arising from an *intensity of personal need and great importance.*

This brings us to the third condition of *diligent study* or *steady, earnest searching.*

Proverbs 2:4 says, "If you seek her as silver, and search for her as for hidden treasures;"

---

[6] James Strong, S.T.D., LL.D., *The New Strong's Complete Dictionary of Bible Words,* introduction by John R Kohlenberger, III, (Thomas Nelson Publishers:Atlanta, London,Vancouver, 1996), 511.

The reference to silver shows the value of what is sought and provides a motive to seek for wisdom when a person desires something of great value. The idea of a hidden treasure suggests that what one is searching for is to be uncovered or discovered by earnest effort.

Thus while one is receiving the word of the LORD with a teachable attitude, and earnestly pouring out his or her soul to God to know the meaning of it, there should also be diligent searching, digging for that precious treasure of wisdom. This is done by actively studying, researching, reading and meditating on the scriptures.

Therefore, if a person is engaged in this way to acquire wisdom, there are two things that will result:

- He or she "will discern the fear of the LORD, and discover the knowledge of God (Proverbs 2:5)
- He or she will "discern righteousness and justice and equity and every good course (Proverbs 2:9).

Why is it that one will discern the fear of the Lord and discover the knowledge of God as a first and primary point? It is because God alone is the source of godly knowledge and wisdom (Proverbs 2:6); and He loves us and cares about how we live on the earth. This is evident by the fact that He guards the steps and the direction of our lives because we fear Him (Proverbs 2:7–8).

Why will a person be able to:

"discern righteousness and justice and equity and every good course" (Proverbs 2:10)?

It is because wisdom will actively enter our hearts. This will have the effect of:

- crowning our thoughts with prudence.
- enabling our minds to discern the truth.
- influencing our affections toward God and holy things.
- creating healthy desires.
- exercising its authority over our feelings.
- guiding our actions.
- conforming our wills to the will of the Holy One.

Indeed, if one does what is suggested in this second chapter of Proverbs, it is inevitable that he or she will grow in the true knowledge of God, and will become a person crowned with a jewel of understanding that marks his or her words and actions (Proverbs 2:11).

And the life of that person will be guarded from the perverse man (Proverbs 2:12-15) and the adulteress woman (Proverbs 2:16–19) because that person will walk in the path of the righteous (Proverbs 2:20).

> "For the upright will live in the land,
> And the blameless will remain in it;
> But the wicked will be cut off from the land,
> And the treacherous will be uprooted
> from it" (Proverbs 2:21, 22).

CHAPTER 2: THREE CONDITIONS OF LEARNING SPIRITUAL TRUTH

How to Find Wisdom, Knowledge, and Understanding	**The Condition of Teachability**	*If* you will receive my sayings —**Listen intently, believe and accept the teaching**	2.1a
		(*If* you will) treasure my commandments within you —**See the great value of the teaching.**	2.1b
		(*If* you will) make your ear attentive to wisdom —**meditate on the teaching.**	2.2a
		(If you will) incline your heart to understanding —**come to know the meaning of the teaching.**	2.2b
	The Condition of Prayer	*If* you cry for discernment	2.3a
		(*If* you) lift your voice for understanding	2.3b
	The Condition of Diligent Study	*If* you seek for her as silver —**as if looking for something valuable.**	2.4a
		(*If* you) search for her as for hidden treasures —**as if to uncover that which is not obvious.**	2.4b
	The Results of Seeking after Knowledge, Wisdom, and Understanding	*Then* you will discern the fear of the Lord.	2.5a
		(Then you) will discover the knowledge of God.	2.5b
		For the Lord gives wisdom, from His mouth comes knowledge and understanding.	2.6-7a
		He is a shield to those who walk with integrity, guarding the paths of justice;	2.7b-8
		Then you will discern righteousness, justice, equity and every good course.	2.9
		For wisdom will enter your heart, knowledge will be pleasant to your soul.	2.10
		Discretion will guard you; understanding will watch over you.	2.11
		To deliver you from the perverse man	2.12-15
		To deliver you from the evil woman	2.16-19
		So you will walk in the way of good men and keep to the paths of the righteous.	2.20
		The end of the upright and the wicked contrasted	2.21-22

QUESTIONS FOR FURTHER STUDY

1. Read Romans 8:5-8. Why is it so important that one guards his or her mind with respect to what one takes into it?

2. If someone says in reference to the word of God, "I have been told that stuff since I was a child, and I already know all about it, and I am done with it!" What do you think might be going on in this person's life?

3. Read Job 28:12-15. Verse 13 says concerning wisdom, "Man does not know its value, nor is it found in the land of the living." To what degree do you understand the value of wisdom? (Try not to answer this too hastily.) How much of your time is spent trying to discover wisdom?

4. We know that the treasures of Christ extend to an unfathomable depth of richness. What are some things you do to develop your understanding beyond surface knowledge to deep treasures?

5. Look again at Proverbs 2:12-15. List the characteristics of the perverse man. Define the word perverse or perversity. What is such a man rejoicing in exactly who "rejoices in the perversity of evil?"

"Wisdom has built her house, she has hewn out her seven pillars;" (Proverbs 9:1)

3

WISDOM'S PILLARS

Read Proverbs 3:1—35.

Godly principles help establish order in a person's life because they help people to govern their behavior by making choices rooted in the immutable character of God Himself. In this chapter there are principles, which I refer to as pillars, upon which wisdom rests. The practice of which will stabilize a person living in a society that has turned its back on God.

The first pillar is OBEDIENCE, that is, *love God with all your heart*. The text starts out with the phrase: "Let your heart keep my commandments."(Proverbs 3:1).

The Hebrew word translated heart is: לֵב transliterated *leb*. It is an important word because it is used 850 times in the Old Testament and is used "very widely for the feelings, the will and even the intellect;"[7]. *Our obedience to God's commands begins in our hearts*. God cares about what is going on in our hearts for the Bible says that He, "searches the hearts"(Romans 8:27),

and again:

> "I the Lord search the heart, I test the mind, even to give
> to each man according to his ways, according to the results
> of his deeds"(Jeremiah 17:10).

---

[7] James Strong, S.T.D., LL.D., *The New Strong's Complete Dictionary of Bible Words*, introduction by John R Kohlenberger, III, (Thomas Nelson Publishers:Atlanta, London,Vancouver, 1996), 400.

The greatest commandment given to us is:

"And you shall love the Lord your God with all your heart and with all your soul and with all your might."(Deuteronomy 6:5).

Proverbs 3:2 teaches that if I should let my heart keep His commandments *it will add years to my life and peace.*

Secondly, we find that there is the pillar of KINDNESS AND TRUTH, that is, *resist hardness of heart.* For it says:

"Do not let kindness and truth leave you; bind them around your neck, write them on the tablet of your heart"(Proverbs 3:3).

We are reminded that "love is patient, love is kind" (1Corinthians13:4). This love is shown in mercy and in truth. Paul said,

"but speaking the truth in love, we are to grow up in all aspects into Him, who is head, even Christ … Therefore, laying aside falsehood, SPEAK TRUTH, EACH ONE *of you,* WITH HIS NEIGHBOR, for we are members of one another." (Ephesians 4:15, 25).

If we do not let loving kindness and truth leave us, *we will find favor with God and men* (Proverbs 3:4).

The third pillar of wisdom is FAITH, that is, *trust the LORD with all your heart.* One of the most popular verses in Proverbs is this:

"Trust in the LORD with all your heart, and do not lean on your own understanding. In all your ways acknowledge Him, and He will make your paths straight" (Proverbs 3:5–6).

This encouraging verse instructs us to trust God—even if there seems to be a conflict in our minds. *God is glorified through it, and we find comfort, peace and guidance* especially when it is hard to understand what is really happening in our lives.

Fourthly, there is the pillar of RIGHTEOUSNESS, which is manifested in *humility,* the *fear of the LORD* and *turning away from evil,* (Proverbs 3:7) especially the evil that is within our own hearts. It is interesting that the passage teaches that *there are health benefits to our bodies* in living humbly and in turning away from evil through the fear of the LORD (Proverbs 3:8).

Wisdom's fifth pillar is that of STEWARDSHIP, which is seen in *honoring God from our wealth*. If we honor God from the things He has given us, then the Lord will honor us with more (Proverbs 3:9–10). This does not mean that we will get more money if we give money, but we will not lack in what we need. The Lord will bless us with plenty *not* so we can spend it on our pleasures, but rather so we can help others with it. We are not the owners of what we have, but the stewards of it.

The sixth pillar is that of TEACHABILITY, that is, that we *do not despise the LORD's correction*. We are warned not to reject the discipline of the LORD (Proverbs 3:11–12). Hebrews 12:9 –10 says:

> "Furthermore, we had earthly fathers to discipline us, and we respected them; shall we not much rather be subject to the Father of spirits, and live? For they disciplined us for a short time as seemed best to them, but He disciplines us for *our* good, that we may share His holiness."

Keep in mind that the discipline we receive from the LORD is a mark of His love for us. This understanding will help us to receive His reproof. When we respond with humility, acknowledging Him, we discover how much grace and lovingkindness He has for us.

By receiving the discipline of the LORD, we *find* (Proverbs 3:13) wisdom and:

- We will see its great profit—it is better than that of gold (vs 3:14).
- We will learn its great value—that nothing we desire can be compared to her (vs 3:15).
- We will discover a long and successful life with blessings (vs 3:16).
- We realize the great peace it brings through her pleasant ways (vs 3:17).
- We will find it to be a tree of life (vs 3:18).
- We will be of the same mind about it as the LORD, for He used wisdom to establish all of creation (vs 3:19–20).

If one receives the discipline of the Lord, that one will *keep* (vs 3:21) wisdom and:

- He or she will find life for his or her soul (vs 3:22).
- He or she will be adorned with beauty (vs 3:22).
- He or she will walk securely (vs 3:23).
- He or she will live without fear (vs 3:24–25).
- He or she will have confidence in the Lord without stumbling (vs 3:26).

The seventh pillar of wisdom is LOVE YOUR NEIGHBOR. There are practical things that you can do to show love to your neighbor.

1. Do not refuse good to your neighbor when you are able to do it (vs 3:27–28).
2. Do not plot to injure your neighbor (vs 3:29).
3. Do not come against your neighbor for no reason (vs 3:30).
4. Do not secretly desire to be like your neighbor if he or she is a violent person (vs 3:31–32).

If you practice love for your neighbor then God will count you as righteous. God blesses the upright in several ways:

- He will draw near to them becoming intimate with them (vs 3:32b).
- He blesses the dwelling of the righteous (vs 3:33b), which suggests that the presence of God is among them.
- He gives grace to the afflicted (vs 3:34b), which shows that the righteous have trouble, but the Lord is there to help.
- He will honor those who fear the Lord (vs 3:35a).

If we do not show love to our neighbor, God counts us as wicked.

- The crooked man is an abomination to Him (vs 3:32a).
- The home of the wicked is cursed suggesting that the presence of the Lord is not there (vs 3:33a).
- God scoffs at the scoffer (vs 3:34a).
- The Lord dishonors the fool (vs 3:35b).

Therefore, love your neighbor.

These pillars of wisdom will help a person to mature who builds his or her life on them, bringing stability and the strength that is so needed in these times.

CHAPTER 3: WISDOM'S PILLARS

Basic Principles of Wisdom's Teaching		
Pillars of the Godly Life	Expected Results	Verse
Love the LORD with All Your Heart: Let your heart keep my commandments. (3:1)	Long life and peace. (3:2)	3:1–2
Resist Hardness of Heart: **(3:3)** • keep kindness • hold on to truth	Favor and a good understanding with God and mankind.	3:3–4
Trust God with All Your Heart: **(3:5)** • Trust in the Lord with all your heart; • acknowledge Him in all your ways.	A clear understanding of God's will and which path to take. (3:6)	3:5–6
Pursue Righteousness: **(3:7)** • Be humble; • fear the Lord • turn away from evil	Healing for your body and refreshment for your bones (3:8)	3:7–8
Stewardship: Honor the Lord from what He has given you. (3:9)	He will honor you. (3:10)	3:9–10

Teachability (Discipleship): Do not reject the discipline of the Lord.(3:11)	1. Realize God's Love (3:12)
	2. Find wisdom; gain understanding (3:13)
	   • Profit (3:14)
	   • Value (3:15)
	   • long and successful life (3:16)
	   • great peace (3:17)
	   • A tree of life (3:18)
	   • The Lord's example (3:19-20)
	3. Keep wisdom and discretion (3:21)
	   • Life to your soul (3:22a)
	   • Beauty (3:22b)
	   • Security (3:23)
	   • Safety (3:24-25)
	   • Confidence in the Lord (3:26)
		3:11–26

Love your Neighbor • Do not withhold good from (3:27–28) • Do not devise harm against (3:29) • Do not contend without cause (3:30) • Do not envy a man of violence (3:31)	God Blesses the Righteous • Closeness in the relationship with God. (3:32b) • Home is blessed (3:33b) • Grace is given (3:34b) • Honor bestowed (3:35b) God Opposes the wicked. • Crooked man is an abomination to God (3:32a) • Home is cursed (3:33a) • God scoffs at scoffers (3:34a) • Dishonor will be evident (3:35b)	3:27–35

QUESTIONS FOR FURTHER STUDY

1. What do you think it means to bind kindness and truth around your neck according to Proverbs 3:3? What do you think it means to write kindness and truth on your heart?

2. How do you acknowledge the LORD in all your ways?

3. Why do you suppose that the scriptures warn us not to lean on our own understanding?

4. Can you recall a time in which you sensed that the LORD was disciplining you? Did you grow with respect to the holiness of God? As you reflect on that time, in what way has your perspective changed — if it has changed at all?

5. What can you do to become more intimate (detailed and deep) with the LORD?

"My son, if your heart is wise, my own heart also will be glad; And my inmost being will rejoice when your lips speak what is right." (Proverbs 23:15–16)

THE BOTTOM-LINE TEACHING
OF A GODLY FATHER

Read Proverbs 4:1—27.

As a father, I think about ultimate outcomes with regard to my children. What are the crucial factors which will shape the direction of their lives? It has been said that we can only do three things.

- We can pray.
- We can be an example.
- We can teach.

Everything else is in God's hands.

I find this statement to be of immeasurable worth. I recognize that in the end my children, who are adults, must make their own choices with respect to their lifelong goals, aspirations and the directions they take. My role as a father has changed since my children have grown up, yet I still have the responsibility as a father to pray and be an example (who knows, maybe they even may ask for advice someday, so I must always be ready to answer them in the right spirit).

Every godly father would desire this: That his children would hate evil, and love righteousness. Turn away from evil and practice godliness. Do the commandments of God and gain the knowledge of the Holy One.

This is why Proverbs 4:7 is such a crucial bottom-line teaching for the children, which says,

"The beginning of wisdom is: Acquire wisdom; and with all your acquiring, get understanding."

Acquiring wisdom and understanding is to be one of life's major pursuits. Such a pursuit holds a promise ultimately of an excellent outcome. Just as it is written in 2 Timothy 3:15:

"and that from childhood you have known the sacred writings which are able to give you the wisdom that leads to salvation through faith which is in Christ Jesus."

The wisdom from the sacred texts is able to lead a person to salvation. And to walk in the salvation that this wisdom gives results in the following:

1. It carries the hope of eternal fruit that brings God everlasting glory.

   "Blessed be the God and Father of our Lord Jesus Christ, who according to His great mercy has caused us to be born again to a living hope through the resurrection of Jesus Christ from the dead, to obtain an inheritance which is imperishable and undefiled and will not fade away, reserved in heaven for you, who are protected by the power of God through faith for a salvation ready to be revealed in the last time."(1Peter 1:3–5).

2. The possessor of this wisdom and understanding has the hope of everlasting joy.

   "In this you greatly rejoice, even though now for a little while, if necessary, you have been distressed by various trials, that the proof of your faith, being more precious than gold which is perishable, even though tested by fire may be found to result in praise and glory and honor at the revelation of Jesus Christ; and though you have not seen Him, you love Him, and though you do not see Him

now, but believe in Him, you greatly rejoice with
joy inexpressible and full of glory, obtaining as
the outcome of your faith the salvation of your
souls."(1Peter 1:6–9).

It cannot not be over-stated that wisdom and understanding is one of
the most valuable possessions of a human being—the obtaining of which
has far reaching effects.

1. It deeply touches inward, personal matters of the heart (Proverbs
   4:4a).
2. Keeping wisdom leads to life (vs 4:4b).
3. It's an issue of hard work and diligence seen as essential in the act
   of acquiring anything of great value (vs 4:5a).
4. It's grounded in the words of the LORD that they should be kept
   with all our heart (vs 4:5b).
5. It depends on the attitude which chooses good and sound teaching
   (vs 4:5).
6. It counters corruption in our souls and helps establish healthy
   affections and pure desires (vs 4:6,8).
7. It becomes to us protection from encroaching evils all around (vs
   4:6a).
8. It brings honor in this life and in the world to come (vs 4:8).
9. It crowns its possessors with beauty and grace (vs 4:9).

Oh how important it is to prize her, to seek her with all your heart,
to willingly welcome, and affectionately and soberly accept wisdom and
understanding!
One of the desirable ultimate outcomes is found in verse 18:

"But the path of the righteous is like the light of dawn,
that shines brighter and brighter until the full day."

This suggests in its context that the righteous and those who acquire
wisdom and understanding are one in the same. One of wisdom's greatest
benefits is that it leads us into upright paths (vs 4:11).

- It is the instruction of wisdom that will keep your feet from stumbling. In the beginning it is like the dawn of the sunrise where light begins to overtake the darkness of the night, and in its practice it only brightens until the full light of day.
- It is the application of the teaching of wisdom that adds years to your life (vs 4:13).
- It is wisdom that instructs us to turn away from wickedness. Proverbs 4:14–15 says:

> "Do not enter the path of the wicked, and do not proceed in the way of evil men. Avoid it, do not pass by it; Turn away from it and pass on."

Implied here is that we each have to face significant decisions in our daily lives. On one hand, we could go in the way of evil men (vs 4:16–17). On the other hand we can go in the way of righteous men. These choices prove our character in the sense that the unknown strength of our character is tested by the choice to do evil or good, and as we choose righteousness, that strength of character is made more certain by the experiential and repetitive choice to do good.

Some of my friends once told me that the whole of life is about the process; and the process we go through is more important than achieving a given end. The choices we make to do right or wrong will manifest the strength or weakness of particular attributes in our lives. The idea is that through the process certain distinguishing qualities or traits are impressed upon our lives, and the sum of these form our character. A person's reputation is made by his or her character.

The outward actions arise from the heart of a person. Thus the bottom-line teaching is to acquire wisdom and understanding. The desired ultimate outcome is a righteous life that is ever increasing in the light of God's Holy Spirit. But to progress in that direction, one must pay attention to the activity of the heart.

How Do These Things Apply?

1. In a most practical instruction, Proverbs 4:20–21 tells us that the words of wisdom and understanding need to be kept in the midst of the heart, that is:
   a) in our minds.

b)   in our affections.
c)   in our desires.
d)   in our feelings.
e)   in our motivations.
f)   in our actions.
g)   in our choices.

God's word is foundational, and must be the most important thing that we take into our inner being.

2.   It is life to those who find them and healing to one's entire body (vs 4:22).
3.   With it, we will be able to set a guard over our hearts, for "from it flow the springs of life"(vs 4:23).
4.   By it we can put away deceitful speech (vs 4:24).
5.   Through it we can show a singleness of mind, and steadfastness of a heart set on following the LORD (vs 4:25).
6.   In response to it, we can turn away from evil (vs 4:27).

In this way we can set an example for our children, and from the storehouse of God's word teach words of wisdom, and know how to pray with the hope that the ultimate outcomes for our children will be bright indeed, inasmuch as it is ultimately in the hands of God.

CHAPTER 4: THE TEACHING
OF A GODLY FATHER

The Surpassing Value of Instruction From a Godly Father	Responding to Godly Instruction	Hear and give attention —Listen, this is how you learn	4.1a
		Do not abandon my instruction.	4.2b
	Motivations for Holding to Instruction	That you may gain understanding	4.1b
		For I give you sound teaching--Stability	4.2a
	The importance of Being a godly Father	My father taught me —more than one generation.	4.3-4a
		Keep my commandments and live —undoubtedly your teaching will reach your grandchildren.	4.4c
	The Bottom Line	Acquire Wisdom —relates to the fear of the Lord (see Proverbs 9:10a)	4.7a
		Acquire Understanding —relates to the knowledge of the Holy One (see Proverbs 9:10b)	4.7b
	Acquiring Wisdom and Understanding —Life's Major Pursuit.	It is a matter of the heart	4.4b
		It is a matter of life and death	4.4c
		It is a matter of hard work, diligent effort.	4.5a
		It is a matter of remembering (the Lord).	4.5b
		It is a matter of choosing good and sound teachings.	4.5c
		It is a matter of healthy affections and desires.	4.6a, 8a
		It is a matter of protection.	4.6b
		It is a matter of honor.	4.8b
		It is a matter of beauty and grace.	4.9
	Dealing with Things Inwardly	It will keep you from the paths of evil	4.10-19
		It will enable you to watch over you own heart springs.	4.20-23
		Always speak the truth.	4.24
		Be single-minded in what you are doing.	4.25
		Be careful, don't be hasty to run down a path.	4.26
		Stick with your convictions, do not allow other men to sway you.	4.27a
		Turn your feet from evil.	4.27b

QUESTIONS FOR FURTHER STUDY

1. The love and knowledge of God is the greatest thing which we can acquire. How is this related to wisdom and understanding?

2. Read Romans 5:3,4. How is character built in our lives? How can we build it in others' lives? How is character important in the leadership of a church? Of a city, state, or nation?

3. Read 2Peter 1:3-11. List the qualities spoken of in this passage. Why are they important to the believer? In making disciples of Jesus Christ, a person must learn knowledge, skills, vision and character. Of these four, why is it that character is the most difficult to impart to people? What does this tell you about the process of making disciples?

4. How can someone know what is the right path to take?

5. How can one keep God's Word in the midst of his or her heart?

"And I discovered more bitter than death the woman whose heart is snares and nets, whose hands are chains. One who is pleasing to God will escape from her, but the sinner will be captured by her." (Ecclesiastes 7:26)

THE SOBERING DANGERS
OF ADULTERY

Read Proverbs 5:1—31.

> Proverbs 5:21 says, "For the ways of a man are before the eyes of the LORD, and He watches all his paths."

The LORD is so great that He is able to see each person on the earth. He sees each individual man, woman and child every moment of every day without exclusion of any person. And He knows us all simultaneously, thoroughly and individually.

Often a person may think that he or she can commit sin in private, and no one will see, no one will know. Such a notion is false indeed, and whoever thinks this way is deceived, for nothing is hidden from God's sight,

> "For My eyes are on all their ways; they are not hidden from My face, nor is their iniquity concealed from My eyes"(Jeremiah 16:17).

Proverbs 5:21 declares that it is the *ways* of a man that are before the eyes of the LORD. The actions we take in fact truly matter to God. The things we do without question count for something with God. However, God sees more than just the deeds of our hands.

Jeremiah 17:9 tells us:

"The heart is more deceitful than all else and is desperately sick; who can understand it?"

Then the LORD says,

"I the LORD search the heart, I test the mind, even to give to each man according to his ways, according to the results of his deeds"(Jeremiah 17:10).

It is the LORD who sees, scrutinizes and knows all that transpires in our hearts, even before we do our deeds. And these things—thoughts, feelings, affections, desires, motives—these matter to the LORD.

We may claim a right to privacy, but in reality, there is no privacy with God. His presence and His knowledge extends to the most secret of places. It encompasses all that goes on in the very soul of a man, woman or child every minute of each day of our lives. It would do us good to meditate on this until we can perceive, even in the smallest measure, the magnitude of His greatness.

God has given us His word if perhaps we might add to it discretion. The very foundation of our lives as believers is to be built upon His word. And from that foundation, we may be able to discern the difference between evil and good, and with that, caution our hearts about what is proper and correct in our conduct.

Peter said:

"seeing that His divine power has granted to us everything pertaining to life and godliness, through the true knowledge of Him who called us by His own glory and excellence. For by these He has granted to us His precious and magnificent promises, in order that by them you might become partakers of *the* divine nature, having escaped the corruption that is in the world by lust. Now for this very reason also, applying all diligence, in your faith supply moral excellence, and in *your* moral excellence, knowledge; and in *your* knowledge, self-control, and in *your* self-control, perseverance and in *your* perseverance, godliness; and in *your* godliness, brotherly kindness, and in *your* brotherly kindness, *Christian* love. For if these *qualities* are yours and are increasing, they render you neither useless nor unfruitful in the true knowledge of our Lord Jesus Christ." (2 Peter 1:3–5).

Peter begins a list of qualities, and at the top of the list is moral excellence. He says of these qualities that not only should we be owners of them, but they should be increasing in us. And if that is the case, we would be both useful to the LORD, and fruitful in our service to God. But if they are not present in our lives, then we must know intuitively that the opposite is true, that is, that we will not be useful nor fruitful.

In the light of what we are meditating on, we come to Proverbs 5:1–2 :

> "My son, give attention to my wisdom, incline your ear to
> my understanding, that you may observe discretion, and
> your lips may reserve knowledge."

Did you notice how Solomon introduced a new teaching by saying something like this: Son, I want you to really listen now, because I am about to give you something that will allow you to possess knowledge, discretion and understanding that may save your life. It requires your attention both to hear and make sense of what I mean when I say what I'm about to say!

Here is a list of references where Solomon is doing something like this:

1. Chapter 1:8–9 He begins to say that we need to listen after he gives us the very key to wisdom.
2. Chapter 2:1–2 He opens the discussion on how to practically obtain wisdom by saying listen to what I am going to tell you now (of course, I am paraphrasing).
3. Chapter 3:1a He again sends a signal to us as readers that He is about to give us something very important—and we discovered wisdom's pillars.
4. Three times in Chapter 4, verses 1, 10, and 20 we are getting a signal that we need to pay attention to what is about to follow.
5. Again in Chapters 6:20; 7:1, 24; 8:32 we see a similar pattern.

So at the beginning of this chapter of Proverbs, we are told to pay attention, because that which follows is significant indeed.

Proverbs 5:3a says, "For the lips of the adulteress"… Immediately, we can see a major area of temptation so powerful and of sin so destructive that it must be brought into view and given the proper attention: the sin of adultery.

It begins with *seduction*. Noah Webster defined seduction in this way:

> *"Appropriately*, the act or crime of persuading a female, by flattery or deception, to surrender her chastity. A woman who is above flattery is least liable to seduction; but the best safeguard is principle, the love of purity and holiness, the fear of God and reverence for his commands."[8]

Notice how the seduction takes place. Proverbs says:

> "For the lips of an adulteress drip honey, and smoother than oil is her speech;"(Proverbs 5:3).

This applies both to the adulteress and the adulterer. His or her words are sweet. They flatter the one they are trying to seduce. Flattery is defined as:

> "False praise; commendation bestowed for the purpose of gaining favor and influence, or to accomplish some purpose."(*Webster*)[9]

This false praise will work on someone whose ego is alive. Someone who has not dealt with self-love is quite susceptible to giving in to false praise. Oh how we need to deal seriously with things inwardly that have to do with self-life. Flattery gratifies those who love themselves.

If someone comes with flattering speech, and you detect it as such, immediately you should be on your guard.

In our day, we speak of people who have smooth words as being "slick." What is meant by that is that they cannot be trusted. There is something deceptive going on. There is trickery taking place. The adulteress, or adulterer, uses deception. They are lying.

---

[8] Noah Webster, LL. D., *An American Dictionary of the English Language*, (S. Converse:New York, 1828, republished in facsimile edition by Foundation For American Christian Education:San Francisco, 1967).

[9] Ibid.

To guard against seduction, you must see through the flattery and deceit. You must look at the consequences of falling prey to those sweet, smooth, words. What you thought was sweet, turns out to be bitter (Proverbs 4:4a). What you thought was so smooth turns out to be sharp (vs 4:4b). And you will discover that you have been robbed. Yes, robbed of life (vs 5:5).

Be on your guard against people who flatter and use deceptive speech. Here is why:

1. It says, "She does not ponder the paths of life;" (vs 5:6a).
   a) An adulterer, or adulteress does not meditate on the things of God. A person must meditate on a matter before he or she can perceive its depth.
   b) They do not know intuitively the truths of God or the mind of God. Intuition is a spiritual function of immediate perception. It does not include the deductive or inductive reasoning of the mind. Because their conscience is defiled, their perception of God has become twisted as well (Titus 3:15).
   c) They do not commune with Him in intimate fellowship, wherein God deals with a person in detail and in depth. These are incapable of true worship (John 4:22–24).
2. It says, "Her ways are unstable, she does not know it" (vs 5:6b). The adulterer and adulteress do not understand their own spiritual condition. They cannot grasp how their conscience is defiled. They cannot walk in uprightness before the LORD .

How is one to avoid falling into the trap of adultery? The first principle is called by many the *distance principle*. Simply put, it means that one should stay far away from the adulteress or adulterer. "Do not go near the door of her house."(vs 5:7–8)

Secondly, *think clearly about the consequences*. They are spelled out for us:

1. Your life, energy and honor goes to others who are strangers (vs 5:9a).
2. Your years go to the cruel one (vs 5:9b).
3. Your strength and wealth goes to strangers (vs 5:10).
4. Your health goes (vs 5:11).

5. And you will suffer deep regret because of the realization of your great folly (vs 5:12-14).

Thirdly, hold to the principle of the *sanctity of sex in the marriage relationship only*. Look how far our nation has fallen. In Noah Webster's day, in 1828, it was considered a crime for a man to use flattery and deception to persuade a woman to surrender her chastity. Today, according to our society, it is okay to have sex with whomever you want if there exists mutual consent between two adults. This is not God's way.

God's way is clear:

1. A married man and woman is to share sexually with their spouse alone (vs 5:15-17).
2. Sexual intimacy between a man and his wife is pure and something about which they can rejoice, and be exhilarated (vs 5:19).

Avoid adultery.

"For why should you, my son, be exhilarated with an adulteress, and embrace the bosom of a foreigner? For the ways of a man are before the eyes of the Lord, and He watches all his paths. His own iniquities will capture the wicked, and he will be held with the cords of his sin. He will die for lack of instruction, and in the greatness of his folly he will go astray."(Proverbs 5:20–23).

CHAPTER 5: THE SOBERING DANGERS OF ADULTERY

The Sobering Dangers of Adultery	How to Identify the Adulterous Woman.	The Firm Foundation of Deliverance	Wisdom and understanding	5.1
			Discretion and knowledge	5.2
		What she Promises	Her lips speak with sweet words of FLATTERY.	5.3a
			Her speech rings with smooth, persuasive DECEPTION.	5.3b
		What She Actually Delivers	Rather than sweet, she turns out BITTER	5.4a
			Rather than smooth, she turns out to be SHARP.	5.4b
			You discovered that she has robbed you of your life, she has taken you to the GRAVE.	5.5
		The True Condition of the Adulterous Woman	She does not ponder the paths of Life.	5.6a
			All her ways are unstable	5.6b
			She is oblivious to her own condition.	5.6c
	How to Avoid the Trap of the Adulterous Woman	The Way of Deliverance	Do not depart from the words of wisdom.	5.7
			The Distance Principle: Stay far away.	5.8
		Realize the Consequences of Moral Failure	Life, energy, and honor goes to others.	5.9
			Wealth goes to strangers.	5.10
			Health goes.	5.11
			You will groan in the realization of your folly.30	5.12—14
		Understand the Proper Fulfillment of God-Given Sexual Desires	Share sexually with your wife alone.	5.15—17
			Rejoice with your wife in the intimacy, and purity of the sexual relationship.	5.18
			Let your wife satisfy your sexual desires; be intoxicated by your wife's love.	5.19--20
		God Will Deal with a Man Who Sins in this Way	God sees the ways of men. WE CANNOT HIDE FROM GOD.	5.21
			There is no exception; sins in this area will capture you.	5.22
			The wicked will die from lack of instruction.	5.23a
			The fool will go astray in his folly.	5.23b

QUESTIONS FOR FURTHER STUDY

1. Besides Proverbs 5:21, find three cross-references that show that God knows a man's ways. Describe your own thoughts about God as you meditate on this.

2. Why is moral excellence so important? How does one increase it in his or her life?

3. What are the four things Noah Webster recommended as a safeguard against seduction?

4. Do you *love* purity and holiness? How does a person come to a place where they love these things?

5. Think of the lostness of the lost, how that their ways are unstable, how that they do not grasp their own spiritual condition due to their own blindness. Spend some time in prayer about them. What is their greatest need? Do you know any such persons? How can you help them?

"For the commandment is a lamp, and the teaching is light; and reproofs for discipline are the way of life," (Proverbs 6:23)

SOME PITFALLS
ALONG THE WAY

Read Proverbs 6:1—35.

This chapter in Proverbs speaks of some pitfalls. One of the realities of the Christian life is that of spiritual warfare. If a believing man or woman is not on the alert, the possibility of falling is great.

One of the reasons for the existence of this war is explained in Galatians 5:16–17. It reads:

> "But I say, walk by the Spirit, and you will not carry out the desire of the flesh. For the flesh sets its desire against the Spirit, and the Spirit against the flesh; for these are in opposition to one another, so that you may not do the things that you please"

Clearly there is a struggle within the ones who are in Christ, who have believed in the redemption that is only in the shed blood of Jesus Christ, in whom the Spirit of God lives. These spiritual battles happen inwardly because in each one of us, who have believed in Christ, the sin nature uses the desires of the flesh to exert its control over our minds, wills and emotions. However, we have been set free from the power of the sin nature through our union with Christ and His death as it is written in Romans 6:3–7:

"Or do you not know that all of us who have been baptized into Christ Jesus have been baptized into His death? Therefore we have been buried with Him through baptism into death, in order that as Christ was raised from the dead through the glory of the Father, so we too might walk in newness of life. For if we have become united with *Him* in the likeness of His death, certainly we shall be also *in the likeness* of His resurrection, knowing this, that our old self was crucified with *Him*, that our body of sin might be done away with, that we should no longer be slaves to sin; for he who has died is freed from sin."

The word "sin" in this passage is not a reference to sins committed. Sins committed is the result of yielding oneself to the desires of the flesh which were energized by the sin nature. Jesus Christ died for our sins committed, and the sin nature was condemned and judged in His own body on the cross. Just as it is written:

"For what the Law could not do, weak as it was through the flesh, God *did*: sending His own Son in the likeness of sinful flesh and *as an offering for sin,* He condemned sin in the flesh, in order that the requirement of the Law might be fulfilled in us, who do not walk according to the flesh, but according to the Spirit." (Romans 8:3–4).

So we have been set free from our former slavery to the sin nature in Christ. This is true because of what God did through Christ's work on the cross. God gave everyone who believes in Christ His Spirit so that we might become partakers of the divine nature. As we are yielding ourselves to the Spirit and walking according to the Spirit rather than according to the flesh we find ourselves experiencing freedom from the power of the sin nature.

Even so, the spiritual battles remain as a reality in the life of a true Christian, and as a result, every believer must remain battle ready because we are living in a fallen world that is full of pitfalls.

The pitfalls referred to here in Proverbs 6 are only a few in the world where there are many. May God give us wisdom to avoid them as we encounter them.

The first pitfall is that snare of becoming a co-signer for someone else's financial obligations, especially a stranger (Proverbs 6:1–5).

- If the neighbor defaults on the loan, it becomes your debt (vs 3).
- The neighbor knows this and thus exercises power over you in as much as he can just not pay (3).

If you come into such a position, go and deliver yourself as quickly as you can.

- Speak with humility to your neighbor, and win his heart to do what is right (vs 3).
- This particular trap may prevent you from being free to serve the LORD if you incur someone's debt.
- It may bind you up for years while you are trying to get your finances right once again.

This relates to spiritual warfare in this way: The motive of being a co-signer may be entirely fleshly on your part, or the purpose of the loan may be to gratify some fleshly desire that will lead to sin. It is wisdom to refuse to be a guarantor for any stranger.

The next trap is that of slothfulness:

> "Go to the ant, O sluggard, observe her ways and be wise, which having no chief, officer or ruler, prepares her food in the summer, and gathers her provision in the harvest. How long will you lie down, O sluggard? When will you arise from your sleep?" (Proverbs 6:6–9).

According to Webster, a sluggard is:

> "a person habitually lazy, idle and inactive;"[10]

These lazy persons are instructed to go to the ant and observe its ways. They labor continuously and without a chief officer or ruler, gathering their

---

[10] Noah Webster, LLD, *An American Dictionary of the English Language* (S. Converse: New York, 1828, republished in facsimile edition by Foundation for American Christian Education: San Francisco, 1985).

provisions. The text is suggesting that this person is lazy because they do not want to get out of bed (vs 9).

The sluggard will suffer poverty because of his failure to work (vs 10–11).

It is possible that a person's fleshly desires can affect his or her motivation so that he or she is not interested in doing anything useful. It's possible that there is a physical or spiritual condition making it a challenge for a person to be encouraged to accomplish something. It is important to discover the cause of a person's lack of desire. The struggle going on here is touching on the person's will.

We can be lazy in the things of God as well. There are basic things that pertain to a life that is useful and fruitful. Some of these very basics are:

1. Supreme love for Christ (Matthew 10:37).
2. Obedience (John 14:21).
3. Prayer (1 Thessalonians 5:17).
4. The Word of God (2 Timothy 3:16–17).
5. Fellowship (Hebrews 10:24–25).
6. Evangelism (2 Corinthians 5:20).

Let's not be idle about these very basic things with what is going on in the world now. Let's put in a steady, earnest effort in the work that God has for us to do. Jesus said to His disciples:

> "Let your light shine before men in such a way that they may see your good works, and glorify your Father who is in heaven." (Matthew 5:16)

The snare of wickedness is a pitfall to be on guard against.

- The wicked man is characterized as a man who communicates his mischief and deceit through gestures (vs 6:12, 13).
- It is said of him that he has perversity in his heart (vs 6:14a).
- He willfully devises evil continually (vs 6:14b).
- He is marked by the fact that he spreads strife (vs 6:14c, 19).
- Such a person will suddenly come to calamity in which he will instantly be broken, and there will be no healing (vs 6:15).

This person has not dealt with the inward things that are listed as the seven abominations to the LORD:

1. He has haughty eyes. This is an *attitude of pride* (vs 6:17a). The scriptures tell us that God is opposed to the proud (James 4:6).
2. He has *deceitfulness in his heart*, for he has a lying tongue (Proverbs 6:17b).
3. He *commits murder*, there is *hatred in his heart*, killing the innocent (vs 6:17c).
4. He has a heart that is engaged in *premeditated and intentional evil* (vs 6:18a).
5. When the opportunity comes, he exhibits a *willful and unhesitant indulgence in evil* (vs 6:18b).
6. He *willfully lies against another person* (vs 6:19a).
7. This person, by spreading *strife among brothers, divides them* (vs 6:19b).

These things the LORD hates (vs 6:16).

Finally, there is the pitfall of adultery. There are three things mentioned in this passage that will help keep you from the adulterer or the adulteress.

1. *The word of the LORD.*
    a) Do not forsake the word of God (vs 6:20).
    b) Bind them continually on your heart (vs 6:21).
        i. Be seriously committed to get God's word in your mind,
        ii. let it be your desire continually.
        iii. Set your affections on the word of God.
    c) Then you will find that "when you walk about, they will guide you; when you sleep, they will watch over you; when you awake they will talk to you. For the commandment is a lamp and the teaching is light; and reproofs for discipline are the way of life." (vs 6:22, 23).
2. *Do not desire her beauty in your heart* (vs 6:25).
    a) Do not covet your neighbor's wife (Exodus 20:17).
    b) Deal with your desires and affections. What is happening inwardly must be governed.
3. *Do not stare at a person's form and beauty* (Proverbs 6:25).
    a) The world says that it's okay to look (Romans 12:2).

    b)   However, the word of God warns us about looking.

    c)   It's the looking that stirs unholy desires and coveting.

4.   *Consider the consequences of this sin:*

- Financially—"one is reduced to a loaf of bread" (Proverbs 6:26a).
- Spiritually—"the adulteress hunts for the precious life" (vs 6:26b).
- Physically—"The one who commits adultery with a woman is lacking sense; he who would destroy himself does it" (vs 6:32).
- Socially—"wounds and disgrace he will find, and his reproach will not be blotted out."(vs 6:33)

These are some of the pitfalls of our spiritual warfare. In our time we need to be soberly aware of the things happening that are coming as destructive forces to destroy us. We must remind ourselves we are in a battle, and be ready for the fight. Ephesians 6:10–13 says:

> "Finally, be strong in the Lord, and in the strength of His might. Put on the full armor of God, that you may be able to stand firm against the schemes of the devil. For our struggle is not against flesh and blood, but against the rulers, against the powers, against the world-forces of this darkness, against the spiritual forces of wickedness in the heavenly places. Therefore take up the full armor of God, and that you may be able to resist in the evil day, and having done everything, to stand firm."

CHAPTER 6: SOME PITFALLS ALONG THE WAY

Pitfalls Along the Path of Life	**Guaranteeing Someone Else's Debt**	The ensnaring circumstances of becoming surety.	6.1, 2
		Deliver yourself by humility and importunity.	6.3
		Be urgent, and diligent about being delivered.	6.4
		Be swift, speedy, or quick about your deliverance.	6.5
	Laziness	The Ant is an object lesson for the sluggard.	6.6-8
		The warning is given to the sluggard.	6.9-11
	Wickedness	The worthless, the wicked man, characterized.	6.12-14
		The recompense of the worthless, the wicked man.	6.15
		The certainty is that there are some things that the Lord hates.	6.16
		Haughty eyes —an attitude of pride.	6.17a
		a lying tongue —sins committed with the mouth, especially deceit.	6.17b
		Hands that shed innocent blood — violent deeds.	6.17c
		A heart that devises wicked plans — premeditated and intentional evil.	6.18a
		Feet that run rapidly to evil —willful and unhesitant indulgence in evil.	6.18b
		A false witness who utters lies —willful lying against another person.	6.19a
		One who spreads strife among brothers —divides brothers	6.19b
	Adultery	The Three Things That Will Keep You From The Adulteress.	6.20-25
		The financial, spiritual, emotional and social consequences of adultery	6.26-35

QUESTIONS FOR FURTHER STUDY

1. How do you deal with laziness? What about procrastination, what motivates you to work on the important things rather than put them off?

2. Proverbs 6:15 says, "Therefore his calamity will come suddenly; instantly he will be broken, and there will be no healing." What is the difference between this instant breaking, and the breaking that happens to godly people?

3. What things must not be done if we are to avoid becoming one who divides brothers and sisters in the body of Christ?

4. Hebrews 4:12 tells us that the Word of God is living and active. How does the Word of God seem to you? Does it talk to you when you awake? Does it guide you when you walk about? How can you increase your interaction with the Word of God?

5. With respect to the things you love, evaluate that upon which you have your affections set. How can you turn your affections towards the Lord?

"My son, keep my words, and treasure my commandments within you. Keep my commandments and live, and my teaching as the apple of your eye." (Proverbs 7:1)

THE NAÏVE LAD

Read Proverbs 7:1—27.

Proverbs 7 opens with an appeal to keep the words, commands and teachings of a godly father as the "apple of the eye." Wisdom is to be viewed as a sister and understanding an intimate friend (Proverbs 7:4). The purpose is: "That they may keep you from an adulteress, from the foreigner who flatters with her words." (Proverbs 7:5).

By implication, the text suggests that keeping the word of God as a central focus of our lives will guard us from committing sexual sins.

In the story of the naïve lad, he proves he is lacking sense because he chooses the way to the adulteress (Proverbs 7:8). *The choices we make show our character to those who are observing our lives.* If the path you choose leads to evil, that choice was foolish.

He is unaware of being watched (Proverbs 7:6–7). *In fact, it is unmistakably true that our lives are watched and known by many people.* We deceive ourselves if we think that no one will know what we are doing. We must not be ignorant of the fact that people are watching our lives even if they do not see us on a daily basis. They will hear of our activities and will know something of what is going on through the grapevine. Not only this, but God Himself is watching, and we cannot escape His scrutiny (Psalm 139:1-4).

The naïve lad is going out in the darkness with the intent to commit sin (Proverbs 7:7b—9). *Whenever a person goes out deliberately to transgress against the divine or human law that one is lacking sense.*

Then a woman comes to him dressed as a harlot. Her character and characteristics are obvious:

- She is licentious (sexually unrestrained) (vs 7:10a).
- She is cunning in that she is intent on executing an underhanded, evil scheme (vs 7:10b).
- She does not remain at home herself because she is unfaithful to her own husband (vs 7:11).
- She is loud and rebellious (vs 7:11).
- She is aggressive and forward (vs 7:13).
- She is crafty and deceptive, pretending to be right with God using religious speech (vs 7:14) .
- She employs flattery to seduce him (vs 7:15).
- She lures him with pleasure appealing to his own desires (vs 7:16–18).
- She gives him a false sense of not being caught (vs 7:19–20).

The naïve lad is easily enticed by her many persuasions:

- He is seduced by her smooth words (vs 7:21a).
- He is deceived by her flattery (vs 7:21b).
- He is overtaken by her skills (vs 7:22).

Abruptly he becomes unrestrained in passion, but a prisoner of sin (Proverbs 7:22).

As James 1:14–15 says:

> "But each one is tempted when he is carried away and enticed by his own lust. Then when lust has conceived, it gives birth to sin; and when sin is accomplished, it brings forth death."

So Proverbs 7:22 says:

> "Suddenly he follows her, as an ox goes to the slaughter, or as *one* in fetters to the discipline of a fool."

He is caught in her trap, but there is a heavy cost, for it says,

"Until an arrow pierces through his liver, as a bird hastens to the snare, so he does not know that it *will cost him his life.*" (vs 7:23).

This is suggesting that he will acquire a sexually transmitted disease, and it will cost him his life.

Thus the conclusion is,

"Do not let your heart turn aside to her ways, do not stray into her paths. For many are victims she has cast down, and numerous are all her slain. Her house is the way to Sheol, descending to the chambers of death" (Proverbs 7:25–27).

How should we respond to the story of the naïve lad?

1. *Be diligent to guard the direction of your heart.* The heart consists of the mind, will and emotions. The things, upon which you set your affections and desires, will lead to what you think about. What you think about turns into action.

Therefore, yield your desires and affections to the control of the Lord.

> Psalm 37:6 says, "Delight yourself in the Lord and He will give you the desires of your heart."

> 2 Corinthians 10:5–6 reads, "We are destroying speculations and every lofty thing raised up against the knowledge of God, and we are taking every thought captive to the obedience of Christ, and we are ready to punish all disobedience, whenever your obedience is complete."

2. *Be careful to stay away from the adulteress.* Avoid the circumstance of being alone with an adulterer or adulteress.

2Timothy 2:22 exhorts us to

> "Now flee from youthful lusts, and pursue after righteousness, faith, love *and* peace, with those who call on the Lord from a pure heart,"

Choose to associate yourself with those who are seeking the Lord daily with all their heart.

3. *Remember that her house is the way to the grave.* Think through the consequences of yielding to the sexual sin of adultery.

Galatians 6:7, 8 says,

> "Do not be deceived, God is not mocked; for whatever a man sows, this he will also reap. For the one who sows to his own flesh shall from the flesh reap corruption, but he one who sows to the Spirit shall from the Spirit reap eternal life."

Again, Galatians 5:19–21 reminds us that our fleshly activities affects life after death saying:

> "Now the deeds of the flesh are evident, which are: immorality, impurity, sensuality, idolatry, sorcery, enmities, strife, jealousy, outbursts of anger, disputes, dissensions, factions, envyings, drunkenness, carousings, and things like these, of which I forewarn you just as I have forewarned you that those who practice such things shall not inherit the kingdom of God."

So then, not only will one reap in this life according to what he or she has sown, but in the life to come one's fleshly practices will have a bearing on one's inheritance with respect to the kingdom of God.

CHAPTER 7: THE NAÏVE LAD

The Naïve Lad and the Adulteress	**The Father's Plea**	Listen, value and obey this word from you father	7.1, 2
		Do not let his word be far from you	7.3, 4
		The teaching has one purpose: to keep you from the adulteress.	7.5
	The Characteristics and Character of the Naïve Lad	He is lacking sense(lit: heart)	7.6--9
		He is easily enticed, seduced, deceived and overtaken. Unrestrained in PASSION, restrained by SIN.	7.21, 22
	The Characteristics and Character of the Boisterous Adulteress	She dresses in appearance as a harlot —LICENTIOUS.	7.10a
		She is cunning of heart —CRAFTY AND SLY.	7.10b
		She does not remain at home —UNFAITHFULNESS.	7.11, 12a
		She lurks---DECEPTIVE AND STEALTHY.	7.12b
		She is LOUD AND REBELLIOUS.	7.11
		She is AGGRESSIVE AND FORWARD.	7.13
		She is BOLD AND SHAMELESS.	7.13
		CRAFTY IN DECEPTION.	7.10--13
		CRAFTILY DECEIVED BY THE EVIL OF HER OWN WAYS	7.10--13
	The Trap of Deception	"I was due to offer peace offerings … I paid my vows"--PRETENSE OF GOOD.	7.14
		"I have come out to meet you" --WORDS OF FLATTERY	7.15
		THE ALLURE OF PLEASURE	7.16--18
		A FALSE SENSE OF NOT BEING CAUGHT	7.19, 20
	The Cost	"AN arrow pierces through his liver"--DISEASE.	7.23a
		"It will cost him his life"--DEATH.	7.23b
	Exhortations and Admonitions	"DO NOT LET YOUR HEART TURN TO HER WAYS"	7.24--25a
		"DO NOT STRAY INTO HER PATHS"	7.25b
		"…MANY ARE THE VICTIMS SHE HAS CAST DOWN"	7.26a
		HER HOUSE LEADS TO THE GRAVE.	7.26--27

QUESTIONS FOR FURTHER STUDY

1. Ephesians 6:11 informs us that the devil employs schemes against the saints. We as Christians are in a battle. There is spiritual warfare that we must face. Consider the adulteress of Proverbs 7:10-13. She is said to be cunning of heart. In what ways do you see a reflection of the schemes of the evil one in her?

2. What elements of the temptation of this naïve lad are similar in general to the majority of temptations we face?

3. At the crucial point of the temptation of this naïve lad, is there a pattern that represents the normal process that we go through that leads to sin?

4. Consider the trap of deception in Proverbs 7:14-20. What elements can be seen here in Satan's schemes?

"Blessed is the man who listens to me, watching daily at my gates, waiting at my doorposts." (Proverbs 8:34)

8

WISDOM CRIES OUT

Read Proverbs 8:1—36.

This most interesting chapter of Proverbs begins with a rhetorical question:

> *"Does not wisdom call, and understanding lift up her voice?"*
> (Proverbs 8:1)

With this wisdom is personified. The personification of wisdom is figurative—an effective literary device to bring forth the truths and significance of wisdom. Since wisdom has its source in the LORD Himself, we can view this chapter as exemplifying the lovingkindness of the LORD reaching out to mankind, and pleading for men to fear the LORD and turn away from evil. For this is the beginning of wisdom in our lives (Proverbs 9:10).

I. Consider how universal is His call to righteousness through wisdom:
    A) In every place one goes throughout the day, wisdom is calling to us (Proverbs 8:3). For example:
        1. The first part of verse 2 says, "On top of the heights beside the way,…" This gives a word picture of being on a mountain top that is in a wilderness area. Down through the years, we have gone to parks that were a place of

solitude and quietness. It is in such places, the wisdom is there, ready to meet us with guidance from the LORD.

2. The second part of verse 2 says, "Where the paths meet, she takes her stand;" These words carry the idea of an intersection of paths going in different directions. Throughout life, we come to places like this. We are going in one direction, and we come to a crossroads, where we have to make important decisions. Wisdom is there as well, and guides us to the best path to take.

3. The first part of verse 3 says, "Beside the gates, at the opening to the city," In the Old Testament times, the gates at the entrance of the city was the place where the leaders and elders of the community did official, legal and public business. This verse is speaking of wisdom calling out to leaders of the city.

4. Verse 8:3b states, "At the entrance of the doors, she cries out:" This word picture brings to mind the idea of something new. At different times, we are presented with new doors of opportunity, or something never before encountered. Wisdom is there ready to guide those who would consult her (vs 8:3b).

B) To every person God makes His offer of wisdom (vs 8:4).

1. To the naïve ones and to the fools He says learn to recognize wisdom (vs 8:5).

2. To those who love her and diligently seek her (vs 8:17).

3. To kings, princes, rulers and judges (vs 8:15–16).

II. The call of wisdom is really an invitation from the LORD to receive something of immeasurable worth:

A) Principles and ideas which are high, lofty and right (vs 8:6a).

B) The most excellent spiritual things of God (8:7–14).

1. Truth (vs 8:7a).

2. Righteousness (vs 8:8a).

3. Counsel is sound wisdom and insight in order to gain strength (vs 8:14)

4. Godly instruction and knowledge (vs 8:10).

C) Straightforward and right things (vs 8:9).

1. full of knowledge (vs 8:10).

2. discretion (vs 8:12)

3. the fear of the Lord (vs 8:13). In the fear of the LORD, there is no crookedness or perversion; there is no pride or arrogance (vs 8:13).

D) Power and influence will be known by those who possess wisdom (vs 8:14).

E) The things wisdom offers are better than gold, silver or jewels (vs 8:11–17).

F) Yes, the most desirable things one can think of cannot be compared to wisdom (8:11).

III. Wisdom's call to mankind is an appeal to turn away from evil.

A) One of the clearest statements about the fear of the LORD and its relationship to turning away from evil is this verse:

> "The fear of the LORD is to hate evil; Pride and arrogance and the evil way, and the perverted mouth, I hate;" (vs 8:13)

B) This is the essential element of wisdom that leads to the knowledge of God, Himself.

The LORD is wisdom's source. He created the entire universe through His wisdom (vs 8:22-31). Men are still studying the universe and have yet to unlock all its mysteries.

Therefore, do not neglect wisdom. The man or woman who takes heed to her instruction daily will be blessed (vs 8:33--34).

> "For he who finds me finds life, and obtains favor from the LORD. But he who sins against me injures himself; All those who hate me love death." (vs 8:35–36).

CHAPTER 8: WISDOM CRIES OUT

The Great Offer of Wisdom	**Wisdom's Call is Universal — in Every Place**	IN PLACES OF SOLITUDE--"ON THE TOP OF THE HEIGHTS"	8.2
		IN IMPORTANT DECISIONS--"WHERE THE PATHS MEET"	8.2
		IN PLACES OF LEADERSHIP--"BESIDE THE GATES,... TO THE CITY."	8.3
		IN THE BEGINNING OF SOMETHING NEW--- "AT THE ENTRANCE OF THE DOORS"	8.3
	Wisdom's Call is Universal — to All Men	TO THOSE WHO LOVE WISDOM	8.17, 21
		TO THOSE WHO SEEK HER WITH DILIGENCE.	8.17
		TO KINGS, RULERS, PRINCES AND NOBLES.	8.15, 16
		TO ALL WHO JUDGE RIGHTLY.	8.16
	Wisdom's Call is an Invitation to Receive Something of Immeasurable Worth	HIGH AND LOFTY THINGS---SPIRITUAL THINGS OF GOD FOR EXAMPLE	8.6
		TRUTH	8.7
		RIGHTEOUSNESS	8.8, 20
		COUNSEL AND INSTRUCTION THAT IS: STRAIGHTFORWARD AND RIGHT, PRUDENT, KNOWLEDGEABLE, DISCRETE, ROOTED IN THE FEAR OF THE LORD	8.10, 14, 6, 9, 5, 12, 13
		POWER	8.14
		BETTER THAN EARTHLY TREASURES	8.10, 11, 19
		ALL DESIRABLE THINGS IN THIS WORLD CANNOT COMPARE TO WISDOM	8.11
	Wisdom's Call is an Appeal to Turn Away From Evil	WICKEDNESS IS AN ABOMINATION TO WISDOM	8.7
		THERE IS NO CROOKEDNESS OF PERVERSION FOUND IN WISDOM.	8.8
		PRIDE, ARROGANCE AND THE EVIL WAY IS HATED BY WISDOM.	8.13
	Wisdom's Heritage	POSSESSED OF THE LORD	8.22
		ESTABLISHED FROM ETERNITY	8.23
		ESTABLISHED BEFORE THE CREATION	8.24-26
		PRESENT DURING THE CREATION	8.27--31
	Results of Those Who Love Wisdom	OBEY TRUTH	8.32
		DO NOT NEGLECT WISDOM, BUT LISTENS FOR IT, WATCHES AND WAITS (OR IS ALERT) FOR IT	8.33--34
		THEY FIND LIFE	8.35
		THEY OBTAIN FAVOR FROM THE LORD	8.35
		LOVES HIMSELF—IN THE GOOD SENSE.	8.36

QUESTIONS FOR FURTHER STUDY

1. It is said that wisdom is crying out to the sons and daughters of men. In what circumstances do you see this happening in your daily experience?

2. To whom does wisdom reach out on a daily basis?

3. How does one acquire wisdom?

4. With respect to creation, what part did wisdom play? What does this say about God's creative activity? How does it measure against the idea of chance plus time plus the impersonal?

5. Think of those things which you desire the most. Do you really believe that wisdom's value is so great that it cannot be compared to those things you desire? In what practical ways can you demonstrate that you truly desire wisdom above those other things which you desire?

"The fear of the Lord is the beginning of wisdom, and the knowledge of the Holy One is understanding." (Proverbs 9:10)

THE FEAST OF WISDOM —
THE COUNTERFEIT OF FOLLY

Read Proverbs 9:1—18.

The Word of God often is compared to food. For example, 1Peter 2:2 says:

> "like newborn babes, long for the pure milk of the word,
> that by it you may grow in respect to salvation."

Milk is a metonymy used to describe a basic comprehension level of God's word. It conveys a certain maturity level. In the beginning of our Christian walk, we were like a newborn child. Every infant starts out with milk rather than meat. This suggests that some of the teachings in the Bible are basic and foundational, while others are difficult to grasp and not for the immature.

It carries the idea of nourishment as well. The milk of the word of God nurtures growth in new and young Christian believers in the knowledge of the things of God.

Another passage employs the same sort of figurative language by saying,

> "For though by this time you ought to be teachers, you
> have need again for someone to teach you the elementary
> principles of the oracles of God, and you have come to need

milk and not solid food. For everyone who partakes only of milk is not accustomed to the word of righteousness, for he is a babe. But solid food is for the mature, who because of practice have their senses trained to discern good and evil" (Hebrews 5:12–14).

This portion of scripture shows us that there is a time when one must go on to solid food. We cannot receive all that we need if we only drink milk. We must go on to sound teachings if we are to mature and become useful in helping others to understand God's principles beyond the basics.

Job tells of the vital importance of the word of God when he declares,

"I have not departed from the command of His lips; I have treasured the words of His mouth more than my necessary food" (Job 23:12).

Just as food is necessary for the survival of life in the world, God's word is necessary for the survival of our spiritual lives in this world. And recognizing this, Job treasured it above the food he ate to sustain his physical life.

Jeremiah says,

"Thy words were found and I ate them, and Thy words became for me a joy and the delight of my heart; For I have been called by Thy name, O Lord God of hosts" (Jeremiah 15:16).

Again we see God's word referred to figuratively as something to be received, chewed on, swallowed and digested. It becomes a part of our own soul, bringing joy and delight in the midst of our thoughts, an anchor to our emotions, a stability in times of trouble, a basis for decisions and choices in life.

Proverbs chapter 9 tells us that wisdom has a feast all prepared for anyone who wishes to partake. It is a banquet like no other you have known. It will:

• Instruct the simple: "Whoever is naive, let him turn in here!" (vs 9:4)

- Enlighten the heart: "To him who lacks understanding she says, 'Come, eat of my food,'" (vs 9:4b—5a).
- Give life: "Forsake your folly and live," (vs 9:6a).
- Guide the feet: "And proceed in the way of understanding." (vs 9:6b).
- Correct those who err : "Reprove a wise man,…" (vs 9:8b).
- Heal the soul: "…, and he will love you." (vs 9:8b).
- Enrich the understanding: "Give instruction to a wise man, and he will be still wiser, teach a righteous man, and he will increase his learning." (vs 9:9).
- Teach the fear of the LORD (vs 9:10a)
- Lead to the knowledge of the Holy One (vs 9:10b)
- Extend one's life: "For by me your days will be multiplied, and years of life will be added to you." (vs 9:11).

But those who enter wisdom's house can expect to be corrected, reproved, instructed and taught. *The kind of person you are is seen in how you respond.* When corrected do you scoff? Or do you love the reproof of wisdom? Are you teachable? Are you correctable? (vs 9:12)

The woman of folly is also calling out to the righteous, to those who are making their way straight (vs 9:15). Yes, the woman of folly also has a feast! Notice the warfare that the righteous face. Realize the proving that godly men and women must undergo.

This personification of folly speaks with deception, and sounds like the master of lies, the author of evil, as if he is speaking through her. Indeed, can there be a greater folly for a Christian than to follow after evil? Her dark drink is referred to as a stolen, sweet beverage (vs 9:17a), but her water is bitter as death (vs 9:18). Her secret bread of evil deeds, and evil teachings, is called by her pleasant (vs 9:17b), but it ends up ruinous to the souls of those who eat it (vs 9:18). She is only thinking of the present, temporary pleasures of this life. There is no eternal perspective in view. She offers instant gratification, sensual enjoyments, temporal entertainments which divert the soul to lesser things. Her poisons drag the mind into the base and earthly things to be engulfed by the intoxicating lusts of the lower nature in mankind, corrupting and making one's heart callous toward the Holy One.

"If you are wise, you are wise for yourself, and if you scoff, you alone will bear it" (vs 9:12).

For those who eat the food of folly will enjoy the fellowship of those on the path of death (vs 9:18).

This chapter is the invitation to the feast that wisdom has prepared. That feast is what follows in the rest of the pages of Proverbs.

O Christian, which feast do you choose?

CHAPTER 9: THE FEAST OF WISDOM —
THE COUNTERFEIT OF FOLLY

The House of Wisdom and the House of Folly	Wisdom Reaches Out	Her Preparations	House of seven pillars — FOUNDATIONAL PRINCIPLES	9.1
			Dinner and table set —A SPIRITUAL FEAST	9.2
		Her Invitation to The Naive	She calls out---FROM THE HEIGHTS OF THE CITY	9.3
			To the naïve, to him who lacks understanding	9.4
			Come and taste of my food	9.5
			Forsake your folly and live	9.6
		Are You Teachable?	Concerning the scoffer	9.7-8a
			Concerning the wise man	9.8b-9
			The Key To Wisdom — KNOWLEDGE OF THE HOLY ONE	9.10-12
	Folly Advertises	Her Character	Boisterous	9.13a
			naive	9.13b
			ignorant	9.13c
		Her Invitation to the Righteous	Sitting by her house	9.14a
			Sitting by the high places of the city	9.14b
			Calling to those who pass by who are making their way straight	9.15, 16
			Her Deception	9.17
			Her Reward--Death	9.18

QUESTIONS FOR FURTHER STUDY

1. What do you think the seven pillars represent in Proverbs 9:1?

2. Wisdom offers correction, reproof and instruction. Consider what 2Tim 3:15, 16 says. How important is it that a person remains correctable and teachable?

3. The text says that both wisdom and folly call out to the naïve. Is there a difference between the naïve of Proverbs 9:4 and the naïve of Proverbs 9:16? If so, what is the difference?

4. Meditate on Proverbs 9:7-9. What is an important consideration when you reprove, correct or instruct someone?

5. How does one gain the knowledge of the Holy One?

A GREAT FEAST OF WISDOM AND UNDERSTANDING

THE PROVERBS OF SOLOMON

"and may be found in Him, not having a righteousness of my own derived from the Law, but that which is through faith in Christ, the righteousness which comes from God on the basis of faith," (Philippians 3:9)

10

WHY ONE SHOULD DESIRE RIGHTEOUSNESS

Read Proverbs 10:1—32.

Compare and contrast are excellent ways to increase one's learning through observation of the similarities and distinctions between two things. Solomon's proverbs in chapter 10 begin by contrasting the righteous against the wicked, and the wise against the foolish. These contrasts enable us to understand why we should choose righteousness which is the theme of this lesson.

Motivations For Choosing Righteousness

I. The Righteous Will Bear The Fruit Of Wisdom
    1. In the relationship with their parents, the righteous will make their fathers glad (Proverbs 10:1a).
    2. In the stewardship of their time, the righteous serve others doing what is needed at the right time (vs10:5a).
    3. With respect to authority, the righteous one is able to receive commands in humility with an attitude of a servant (vs 10:8a).
    4. The wise (righteous one) possesses knowledge which is able to edify, encourage and help others (vs 10:14a).
    5. The righteous restrains his or her lips in order to avoid transgressions (vs 10:19).
    6. The righteous enjoy doing wisdom (vs 10:23).

In all the above, the fruit of righteousness is the same as the fruit of wisdom. Why? One who is wise fears the LORD and has knowledge of the Holy One. Therefore, you can expect that the one who fears the LORD will live in a way that honors Him.

II. The Righteous Prolongs His or Her Life.
1. It tells us that righteousness will deliver us from death (vs 10:2b).
2. Because the righteous listen to instruction, they demonstrate that they are also on the path of life (vs 10:17a).
3. The fear of the Lord will prolong life (vs 10:27a).

No one knows how long their life will last, but it is abundantly clear that righteousness leads a person away from the paths of death. Through sin death works in the body (Romans 8:13) but the one who lives according to the Spirit truly lives (Romans 8:5-8).

III. The Righteous Bless Other People Through Their Speech
1. The righteous person being crowned with blessings give blessings (Proverbs 10:6).
2. The righteous speak words that are a fountain of life to those who hear (vs 10:11a).
3. A righteous person's speech is characterized with wisdom. (vs 10:13a, 31a).
4. The words of a righteous person is of great value, for it says, "The tongue of the righteous is as choice silver." (vs 10:20a).
5. The words of the righteous are nourishing (vs 10:21a).
6. The word of the righteous is acceptable (vs 10:32a).

When you meet a righteous person, he or she will distinguish themselves by excellent speech. What he or she says rises above what is profane, vulgar or coarse, and imparts healthy, life-giving edification.

IV. The Righteous Obtain An Enduring Integrity.
1. They will know the outcome of a diligent character (vs 10:4b).
2. They will know the blessing of a godly reputation among men (vs 10:7a).
3. They will know the stability of the life of integrity (vs 10:9a)
4. They will produce the results of love (vs 10:12b).
5. They will understand the blessing of the spiritual reservoir of the LORD (vs 10:22).
6. They will know the joy of realized godly desires (vs 10:24b).
7. They will know the security of an eternal foundation (vs 10:25b).
8. They will not be a stranger to the blessing of joy because of the hope he or she possesses (vs 10:28a).
9. The upright will be acquainted with the strength found in the way of the LORD (vs 10:29a).

> The righteous person understands the source of his or her strengths, and does not depart from it, but maintains his or her course in the way of the LORD. He or she walks with the LORD day and night, remembering that the "path of the righteous is like the light of dawn that shines brighter and brighter until the full day" (vs 4:18).

Motivations For Avoiding Wickedness

I. The Wicked Bring Forth The Fruit Of Folly
1. Because of their foolishness, they bring grief to their parents (vs 10:1b).
2. They tend to be given to continual talking, saying too much with little purpose, eventually coming to ruin because of their mouth and unteachable heart (vs 10:8b).
3. They can expect more severe correction because of their lack of *heart* (vs 10:13b). Most versions translate the phrase "lack of heart" as "void of understanding." These wicked ones have a problem in their soul.

4.   Because of hatred in their hearts, slander pours out, but it is obvious to the righteous that they are lying, revealing the true folly of their wickedness (vs 10:18).

5.   But the wicked are entertained by what they are doing not realizing that they are showing themselves to be the fools that they have become (vs 10:23a).

II.   The Wicked Shortens His Or Her Life

1.   The text says, "Ill-gotten gains do not profit." (vs 10:2a) However, the Hebrew literally says "The treasures of wickedness do not profit." In the parallelism of this verse, the implication is that those ill-gotten treasures of the wicked will not deliver them from death. The principle is found in vs 10:27b, "The fear of the LORD prolongs life, but the years of the wicked will be shortened." One cannot be more clear than this.

2.   Proverbs 10:25 likens the lives of the wicked to a whirlwind. Once it passes, they are no more.

III.   The Wicked Cause Trouble And Strife With Their Speech

1.   Like the devil who corrupted his wisdom through the pride of his heart (Ezekiel 28:17), so the wicked cause trouble using the same deceitful tactics of the evil one (Proverbs 10:10, 18) causing strife among people (vs 10:12a).

2.   The divisiveness of their conduct brings ruin (vs 10:14).

IV.   The Wicked Will Not Succeed

1.   Their legacy will disappear for their name will rot (vs 10:7b)

2.   They allow money or the lack of money to be their focus and their trust and are ruined (vs 10:15).

3.   Their worst fears will be realized (vs 10:24a).

4.   Their expectation will perish (vs 10:28b).

5.   They will cease to exist (vs 30:b).

6.   For their perversity will be uncovered (vs 10:9b, 31b),

Therefore, O Christian, choose righteousness in your daily walk.

CHAPTER 10: PART 1—WHY ONE SHOULD DESIRE RIGHTEOUSNESS

Motivations for Choosing Righteousness	**The Righteous Bear the Fruit of Wisdom**	The wise son makes his father glad	1a
		The wise son is not lazy	5a
		The wise heart receives commands —is teachable	8a
		wise men store up knowledge —knowledgeable	14a
		he who restrains his lips is wise — controls speech, bridles tongue	19b
		Doing wisdom is like a sport to the man of understanding —he enjoys wisdom.	23b
	The Righteous Prolongs His/ Her Life	But righteousness delivers from death	2b
		He is on the path of life who heeds instruction,	17a
		The fear of the Lord prolongs life	27a
	The Righteous Blesses Others Through His/ Her Speech	Blessings are on the head of the righteous	6a
		The mouth of the righteous is a fountain of life	11a
		Speaks with discernment/wisdom flows	13a
		What he/she says has great value	20a
		The lips of the righteous speaks nourishing words	21a
		The lips of the righteous brings forth wisdom with acceptable words	31a, 32a
	The Righteous Obtain an Enduring Integrity	The outcome of diligent character	4b
		The blessing of a good reputation	7a
		The stability of a life of integrity	9a
		The results of LOVE	12b
		The blessing of God's spiritual reservoir	22a
		The joy of realized godly desires	24b
		The security of an eternal foundation	25b
		The blessing of joy because of the hope he/she possesses	28a
		The strength found in of The Way Of The Lord	29a, 30a

CHAPTER 10—PART 2: WHY ONE SHOULD DESIRE RIGHTEOUSNESS

Motivations for Avoiding Ungodliness	**The Wicked Bear the Fruit of Folly**	They bring grief to their parents	1b
		They are lazy bringing shame	5b
		They possess a babbling mouth and an unteachable heart	8b
		They lack understanding	13b
		They slander others	18b
		They delight in wickedness	23a
	The Wicked Shortens His/Her life	ill-gotten gains destroy that life which would have been more profitable than the so-called gains.	2a
		The wicked fail to build an eternal foundation living only for the moment they are gone with their whirlwind lives.	25b
		The wicked refuse to revere the Lord and turn away from evil thus their years are shortened.	27b
	The Wicked Causes Trouble and Strife with Their Speech	The Use Of Deceit	10a, 18a
		The Inciting Of Strife Through Hatred	12a
		Their speech brings about ruin.	14b
		They cannot avoid transgression with their many words.	19a
		Their words have little value	20b
		Their mouths speak perversions.	31b, 32b
	The Wicked Are Completely Unstable	Their name will rot	7b
		Their perversity will be discovered.	9b
		Their fears will be realized.	24a
		They are unreliable	26
		Their expectation will perish	28b
		They will cease to exist.	30b

QUESTIONS FOR FURTHER STUDY

1. Proverbs 10:2 states that "Ill-gotten gains" do not profit. This could be translated as, "The treasures of wickedness do not profit, but righteousness delivers from death." The idea of gain from wickedness is here. But this gain does not profit. Why is this so?

2. In Proverbs 10:3 in the Hebrew language, the word for soul is there. One could therefore translate the verse, "The LORD will not allow the soul of the righteous to hunger." What do you hunger for in your soul? How does your hungering in your soul compare to your physical hunger? Where do you go to satisfy the desires of your soul?

3. The word translated "hand" and associated with negligent in Proverbs 10:4 is speaking of a closed hand in the Hebrew. The word translated "hand" and associated with diligent in the same verse is a different word in the Hebrew and refers to an open hand. What does this suggest to you?

4. The word translated negligent in Proverbs 10:4 in the Hebrew means slacking, deceit, fraud. The word translated diligent in the same verse means decision, sharpness. What further insight does this lend to this verse?

"And the seed whose fruit is righteousness is sown in peace by those who make peace." (James 3:18)

LIVING RIGHTEOUSLY
IN EVERYDAY LIFE

Read Proverbs 11:1—31.

Titus 2:11-13 says,

> "For the grace of God has appeared, bringing salvation to
> all men, instructing us to deny ungodliness and worldly
> desires and to live sensibly, righteously and godly in the
> present age, looking for the blessed hope and the appearing
> of the glory of our great God and Savior, Christ Jesus;"

Even though salvation has been made available to all mankind, not
all of mankind is saved because not all mankind believes (John 3:18). If
anyone wishes to have eternal life and forgiveness of sins, that one must
believe in Jesus Christ in order to appropriate this salvation. This is God's
grace toward all who believe.

This grace also teaches us, who have entered into it, that we should say
no to ungodliness and say no to worldly desires. Instead, we are to press
forward to a spiritual life expressed through sensible, righteous and godly
living. This is the believer's love toward God and his or her neighbor.

The motive for living this kind of life as a believer, is that we might
enjoy the fellowship of God and of the saints, walking in love.

Living righteously in and of itself is not sufficient to obtain the
salvation of our souls, or to partake in the Divine nature. The Holy Spirit

of God lives in everyone who believes in Jesus. We are made right with God not because we live in a righteous manner, but only on the basis of grace through faith (Ephesians 2:8–9).

If Jesus Christ had not paid the price that no man or woman could pay, then salvation would be impossible for mankind. It is His shed blood that revealed God's love and grace. It is our response of faith to His shed blood that seals us with the Holy Spirit (Ephesians 1:13–14). We are then made right with God through finished work of the Lord Jesus Christ.

We, as believers, draw upon that Divine nature through the indwelling Holy Spirit, as we present our bodies as instruments of righteousness to Him (Romans 6:13; Romans 12:1) and renew our minds to be transformed by His word into the spiritual people He wants us to be (Romans 12:2). Then we will find ourselves being conformed to Christ rather than the world.

If we however, as believers in the Lord Jesus Christ, continue to present our bodies to the sin nature and do not yield our minds to be renewed, then we will remain conformed to the world in our present state. Even though we are saved, we will be out of fellowship with God and with the saints—not walking in love (1 John 2:15; James 4:4).

The Nature Of Righteousness

Proverbs Chapter 11 gives us an understanding of what a sensible, righteous and godly life looks like. Right from the beginning we learn that God watches all aspects of our lives:

1. He looks at our business transactions to see if there are honest dealings there. Dishonesty in business is completely inappropriate for a Christian and to God it is an abomination (vs 11:1). Some try to separate their business from their Christianity. In doing so they greatly err. We are to walk with God in every aspect of our lives. We are to walk in truth. It may cost money to be honest, but your character is infinitely more important than money.
2. We find that a righteous, godly and sensible life is marked by humility (vs 11:2). There is no one more humble than God, and He sees our heart's attitude whether or not there is pride. The more humility I display, the more I have become like Him. It is written that "God is opposed to the proud" (James 4:6).

3. The righteous are marked by integrity, which guides them (Proverbs 11:3) in all their decisions. Since we know that God will judge our works someday, we must know that He sees the quality of our works as to their character.

4. The righteous do not put their trust in riches but have learned to trust in the LORD. Having an abundance of material things will not help a rich man in the day of judgment (vs 11:4, 28). But the righteous will flourish because of the life that comes from God, which is in them.

> Jesus said: "Beware, and be on your guard against every form of greed; for not even when one has an abundance does his life consist of his possessions." (Luke 12:15)

> The Lord knows whether or not we trust Him, or our riches.

5. The righteous are faithful when it comes to private, personal matters, and therefore can be trusted with confidential information. The Lord will call us to account for unfaithfulness in speech. Love does not broadcast things that should be kept secret (Proverbs 11:12–13).

6. When advice is needed, they seek out wise counsel (vs 11:14). The Lord scrutinizes out steps and is aware of what men have said to us.

7. The righteous are good stewards of their money and possessions, exercising discretion (vs 11:15).

8. They are gracious and merciful with positive results (vs 11:16–17).

9. They walk with pure motives and are generous (vs 11:23–27).

This is not exhaustive, but a summary of a life that is called sensible, righteous and godly. Realize that God manifests His presence and activity in people who live this way so that in them there is a reflection of His power and glory. This is called grace.

The Rewards Of Righteousness

Be assured, such a righteous life will be rewarded by God:

1. The reward for living righteously is not only realized in the life to come, but is also manifested through the sovereign superintending of God over our present lives as well (vs 11:18, 31).
2. He or she, who is godly, will be delivered from death on the day of judgment (vs 11:4).
3. He or she, will be delivered from trouble by his or her righteousness (vs 11:5–6, 8, 21). We are not promised a trouble free life, but He is present in the midst of our trials and He will rescue us from our testings. Just as it is written:

> "And not only this, but we also exult in our tribulations; knowing that tribulation brings about perseverance; and perseverance, proven character; and proven character, hope; and hope does not disappoint; because the love of God has been poured out within our hearts though the Holy Spirit who was given to us. For while we were still helpless, at the right time Christ died for the ungodly. For one will hardly die for a righteous man; though perhaps for the good man someone would dare even to die. But God demonstrates His own love toward us, in that while we were yet sinners, Christ died for us. Much more then, having now been justified by His blood, we shall be saved from the wrath of God through Him." (Romans 5:3–9).

4. He or she will be delivered by knowledge from the ones who slanders and plots against them (Proverbs 11:9).
5. The righteous person will gain favor among the people (vs 11:10).
6. The righteous to attain to life (vs 11:19).
7. The righteous will become like a tree of life to others (vs 11:30).

The Consequences Of Wickedness

The wicked will not get away with the evil which they practice,

1. Dishonor is awaiting them rather than honor (vs 11:2a).
2. The wicked will be destroyed (Proverbs 11:3b—Note that it is the very things they practice which turn out to be what destroys them).
3. When they perish, people will rejoice rather than mourn their passing (vs 11:10b).
4. The wicked have deceived themselves, thinking that they are prospering (vs 11:18a).
5. They live in darkness which results in death (vs 11:19b).
6. God will reward the ungodly for their wickedness in this life (vs 11:21a, 31b).
7. In the depths of their soul they find themselves wanting (vs 11:24b).
8. They have neglected the most important things. In the end, they will inherit emptiness (vs 11:29a).
9. In the life to come the ungodly can also expect to suffer loss (1 Corinthians 3:10–13).

If we desire to walk in love and fellowship with the saints of God and with the Lord Himself as a Christian, then we must deny ungodliness and worldly desires. We must live righteously and godly in this life. This is the way to live sensibly. This is wisdom.

CHAPTER 11: THE CHARACTERISTICS OF THE RIGHTEOUS AND THE WICKED

The Characteristics of the Righteous and the Wicked	Living Righteously in Everyday Life	The Nature of Righteousness	Honesty in business transactions	1b
			Humility	2b
			Integrity will guide them	3a
			Faith in God rather than riches	4, 28
			Without reproach	5a, 20b
			Trustworthy in private, personal matters	13
			Seeks out and listens to wise counselors	14
			Cautious about cosigning for a stranger	15
			Gracious / Merciful	16, 17
			Pure Motives	23, 27
			Generous	24–26
		The Rewards of Righteousness	Deliverance from death	4b
			Deliverance from trouble	5a, 6a, 8a, 21
			Deliverance from slander	9b
			People rejoice over the successes of the righteous	10
			Inherits a true reward	18
			Attains life	19
			A tree of life to others	30
			Their reward is assured	31
	The Wickedness of the Unrighteous	The Nature of Wickedness	Deceit in Business Transactions	1a, 3b
			Pride	2a
			Greed	6b, 28a
			Slanderous	9a, 12
			Untrustworthiness in Private, Personal Matters	13
			Seeks no guidance	14
			Violent	16
			Cruel	17
			Perversity in heart	20
			Impure Motivations	23, 27
			Stinginess	24, 25, 26
			Trouble-Making	29

			Dishonor	2b
			Wrath	4a, 23
			Ensnared	6b
			Without Hope	7
			Trouble	8
			Destroys—Be Destroyed	3b, 9a, 11
	The Wickedness of the Unrighteous	The Consequences of Wickedness	People Rejoice When the Wicked Perish	10
			Deceptive Wages	18
			Death	19
			Leaves in Want	24
			Inherits Emptiness	29a
			Becomes a Servant to the Wise-Hearted	29b
			Will not Get Away With Evil	21, 31

QUESTIONS FOR FURTHER STUDY

1. Jesus told those who were His disciples to choose the narrow way in Matthew 7:13, 14. Can a Christian be on the path to destruction in his or her life?

2. List the traits of wickedness that are found in Proverbs 11. Can a Christian ever be in danger of exhibiting these traits?

3. A beautiful woman who lacks discretion, literally taste, is like a ring of gold in the snout of a swine. How does a woman develop taste?

4. Proverbs 11:30 says, "The fruit of the righteous is a tree of life, and he who is wise wins souls." Describe this fruit, and tell how it wins souls.

5. Proverbs 11:11 says, "By the blessing of the upright a city is exalted, but by the mouth of the wicked it is torn down." In what way can the Christians in America exalt our nation?

"Anxiety in the heart of a man weighs it down, but a good word makes it glad." (Proverbs 12:25)

12

COUNSELING — A PAINSTAKING LABOR OF LOVE

Read Proverbs 12:1—28.

> "The righteous is a guide to his neighbor…" (Prov. 12:26).

In Romans 2:17–21, the Apostle Paul addressed the Jew and said,

> "But if you bear the name 'Jew,' and rely upon the Law, and boast in God, and know His will, and approve the things that are essential, being instructed out of the Law, and are confident that you yourself are a guide to the blind, a light to those who are in darkness, a corrector of the foolish, a teacher of the immature, having in the Law the embodiment of knowledge and of the truth; you therefore who teach another, do you not teach yourself?"

Listen to those words:

> "a *guide* to the blind, a *light* to those who are in darkness, a *corrector* of the foolish, a *teacher* of the immature." (Romans 2:19–20).

How does one arrive at the place in his or her life where he or she becomes such a guide, light, corrector and teacher?

It says that they first "rely upon the Law" (vs 2:17b).

Secondly, they "boast in God"(vs 2:17c).

Thirdly, they "know His will" (vs 2:18a).

And Finally, they "approve the things that are essential" (vs 2:18b).

And how do they accomplish this? It is because they are "instructed out of the Law" (vs 2:18c).

Jesus taught His disciples that they were not only "the salt of the earth," but the "light of the world" (Matthew 5:13–16). And the world needs light. This light comes from the very life (John 1:4) of our Lord and Savior Jesus Christ. This is a Life that is manifested through a believer who is yielded to the indwelling Spirit of God.

How well are you doing at being a guide to your neighbor?

There are a few principles in Proverbs 12 that by inference can be applied to this area of ministry. These I have grouped together in three categories:

- Preparation for counseling.
- Principles in counseling.
- Personal Peace of counseling.

Preparation for counseling

It is quite fitting that we should be reminded that the beginning of knowledge is the fear of the LORD. In Proverbs 1:7, we saw that what was implied is that the one who despises instruction, who despises wisdom, also does not fear the LORD.

In Proverbs 12:1, we find that the one who loves instruction (discipline), loves knowledge. This signifies that the one who loves instruction and who loves knowledge is the same person who listens to reproof. This is the kind of person who is both able to receive instruction and to give counsel.

The love of knowledge and the fear of the LORD are factors in the whole matter of being a light to those in darkness. If we do not allow ourselves to be instructed out of the word of God, if we do not teach ourselves and allow ourselves to be conformed to the truth, we lose credibility in what we say.

Thus the quality of counsel given to someone can be measured by the character of the counselor. To the degree that the counselor allows God's

Word to work in his or her own heart, in the middle of ones own struggles, to that degree, that person will become a more capable counselor.

Thus, the counselor must undergo preparation. Most of this preparation is in the hands of a sovereign God who takes a yielded sinner and forms him or her into a useful and fruitful vessel. They have learned through the fear the LORD to cooperate with Him in His will.

Does this mean that a carnal Christian cannot say the things that are right? No. A carnal Christian can say the things that are true. But such a Christian cannot touch on the spiritual matters (1 Corinthians 3:1–2). He or she is limited because he or she is carnal. By definition, a carnal Christian does not fully attain to the fear of the Lord because they are fleshly in their attitudes and conduct. For this reason, they are not able to be the kind of guide that their neighbor needs to have. You cannot take a person to a place where you have never been.

Remember the words of our LORD who said that

"the mouth speaks out of that which fills the heart" (Matthew 12:34).

A person who is able to deal faithfully with the one coming to him or her for help, is one who is faithfully dealing with the issues in his or her own heart first.

Principles In Counseling

There are a number of principles that are involved in counseling another, but perhaps the number one principle is that a counselor should have the ability to distinguish between the things which differ.

"A man will be praised according to his insight"(Proverbs 12:8).

And this is because with insight he or she is able to shed light on and help solve problems.

Such a person will more than likely manifest the following traits:

1. He or she will determine the facts and give a just reply. (vs 12:5). The word *just* has a number of definitions. Noah Webster wrote

one of the definitions this way: "Conformed to truth; exact; proper; accurate; as just thoughts; just expressions; just images or representations"[11] The next definition reads like this: "True; founded in truth and fact;"[12] A righteous counselor reasons from the facts and his answer is exact, proper and accurate.

2. He or she will be objective without having formed any preconceived bias. For it says, "He who speaks truth tells what is right,..." (vs 12:17). Truth is not arbitrary or prejudiced, but reasonable and without hypocrisy. (James 3:17)

3. He or she will bring an answer that does not compromise the truth (vs 12:17, 22). As a godly counselor, you should be committed to honesty and speaking the truth. Remember what Jesus said in John 8:31-32, "If you abide in my word, you are truly my disciples, and you shall know the truth and the truth shall set you free." You must not tickle the ears or try to be a man pleaser.

4. He or she will listen to the person who is opening up to them. Rash words are words "uttered or undertaken with too much haste or too little reflection."[13] It is not wise to give an answer in haste or with too little reflection. A counselor who is rash, will tend to wound rather than heal. Be a person who *listens* for the meaning of the words being spoken, who sees and understands the heart, and who will be able to guide his or her neighbor to a place of healing. (Proverbs 12:18)

5. He or she will be diligent to bring to light only that which is needed to be known and understood by the one seeking advice (vs 12:23, 27). Most people don't need a lecture, but a clear understanding of what pertains to them. A diligent counselor seeks to present only that which pertains to the matter at hand according to the need of the moment. It will be a precious treasure to him or her.

6. He or she will pinpoint the precise problem. It says that "anxiety in the heart of a man weighs it down, but a good word makes it glad. (vs 12:25) That good word has to be appropriate to the anxiety in order to have the effect of making the anxious heart glad.

---

[11] Ibid.

[12] Ibid.

[13] Noah Webster, LL. D., *An American Dictionary of the English Language*, (S. Converse:New York, 1828, republished in facsimile edition by Foundation For American Christian Education:San Francisco, 1985).

7. In addition to being able to identify the problem, He or she will bring an answer that builds up (vs 12:25). If your neighbor is weighed down with anxious thoughts, as a godly counselor, you will be able to impart a good word that will strengthen and give hope to your neighbor so that the weight is lifted.

8. The scripture says, "But the precious possession of a man is diligence" (vs 12:27b). The godly person never gives up as long they see a response in the one receiving guidance. Diligence is a steady, earnest effort. Diligent counselors stick with their neighbors as long as their neighbors maintain a teachable spirit.

9. He or she will always protect the reputations of people who confide in them (vs 12:16b, 23). This is a matter of wisdom, faithfulness and love. There must be confidentiality maintained in private matters.

Personal Peace Through Counseling

Proverbs 12:20 tells us that "counselors of peace have joy."

1. Perhaps the joy comes from seeing how truth triumphs over the deceitfulness of wickedness (vs 12:7).

2. Or, to see the spiritual fruit that God brings in another person you have counseled (vs 12:12, 26).

3. Perhaps the joy of the counselor of peace is to see how people through faithful dealings were delivered from trouble by the wisdom God supplied (vs 12:13, 21).

4. Perhaps the greatest joy is to see how God heals a person (vs 12:18).

5. Perhaps the joy is in the fact that you learned the ways of love in the whole process.

If you are a guide to your neighbor, be one that invests in them those eternal things that bring everlasting fruit.

CHAPTER 12: COUNSELING — A PAINSTAKING LABOR OF LOVE

Counseling Principles	Factors Which Determine the Quality of Counsel	ONE'S ATTITUDE TOWARD DISCIPLINE	1a
		LOVE OF KNOWLEDGE	1a
		QUALITY OF CHARACTER	26a
		WILLINGNESS TO DEAL FAITHFULLY	1b, 22b
		THE FEAR OF THE LORD	22
	The Rewards of Godly Counsel	WISDOM	15
		FAVOR FROM GOD	2, 22
		STABILITY	3, 7
		JUSTNESS, RIGHTNESS—THE TRUTH WINS	5
		HONOR FROM MEN	8
		REAL SPIRITUAL FRUIT	12, 26
		ESCAPE FROM TROUBLE	13, 21
		SATISFIED WITH GOOD	14
		HEALING	18
		UNFAILING FAITHFULNESS	19
		JOY	20
		ETERNAL LIFE	28
	Skills in Counseling	THE ABILITY TO DISCIPLINE	1
		DETERMINE FACTS, ANSWER WITH CORRECTNESS	5
		LISTENING	18
		BEING OBJECTIVE	17
		PROTECTING THE REPUTATION OF OTHERS	16
		UNCOMPROMISING	17, 22
		THE ABILITY TO LISTEN TO OTHER PEOPLE"S ADVICE	15
		SAY ONLY WHAT IS NECESSARY	23
		PINPOINT EXACT PROBLEM	25
		BRING AN ANSWER THAT BUILDS UP	25
		DILIGENCE--IN DEALING WITH A GIVEN ISSUE, NEVER GIVE UP	27

QUESTIONS FOR FURTHER STUDY

1. What part does the Word of God play in enabling one to be a guide to his or her neighbor?

2. What part does understanding God's will play in being a faithful guide to his or her neighbor?

3. If you are to be a teacher of the immature, what does that imply which must be true for you?

4. If you are to be a teacher of the mature, what do you think that implies which must be true for you?

5. How would you define natural maturity? How would you define spiritual maturity? Is there a difference between natural maturity and spiritual maturity? What is it?

"There is one who pretends to be rich, but has nothing; another pretends to be poor, but has great wealth." (Proverbs 13:7)

TRUE PROSPERITY

Read Proverbs 13:1—25.

"Adversity pursues sinners, but the righteous will be rewarded with prosperity" (Proverbs 13:21).

In the above text, the idea of adversity pursuing the sinner is held in contrast to the notion of the righteous being rewarded with prosperity. This adversity, a *condition of distress,* is not necessarily speaking of a *state of financial misfortune.*

On the other hand, the *condition of prosperity* which is the reward of the righteous, does not preclude the experience of calamity in this life. We live in a fallen world, and the righteous are not exempt from trouble.

Christianity is despised because we say people, in the natural state after the Fall, are inherently evil. We say that mankind's basic problem is that all are sinners. Thus all are in need of a Savior. There is only One who qualifies to be the Savior of mankind, the sinless One, the Lord Jesus Christ. Because of His great love, He stood in the place of all mankind and bore the sins of the world in His own body on a Roman cross. On the third day, He rose again from the dead so that whoever believes in Him might be forgiven of the sins committed by them. They are justified by faith and receive God's gift of eternal life through the entrance of and union with the Holy Spirit who comes into their lives.

If anyone makes an "advance or gain in anything good or desirable,"[14] that one is said to have prospered. This is where the righteous prosper: Those who are yielded to the Holy Spirit, are always making advancement in turning away from evil, in doing God's will and increasing in the knowledge of the Holy One.

Prosperity comes when people, conditions and circumstances contribute together to what is positive for the attainment of a particular good. For example:

1. When a father disciplines his children and they accept their father's discipline by doing what their father instructed them to do, then the father is prospering with respect to his children's advancement into wisdom (vs 13:1).

2. When one guards his or her speech, his or her life is preserved, delivering them from evil (vs 13:3).

3. If a person applies himself or herself diligently in what they are doing, in their soul they will be filled with satisfaction when they achieve their goal (vs 13:4, 19).

4. When the light of the life of the righteous shines brightly, the righteous has a brilliant hope (vs 13:9).

5. If the righteous does not presumptuously do whatever they want to do, but rather consider wise and good counsel, their choices will line up with whatever God's will is (vs 13:10).

6. When the righteous work hard at doing God's will to bring into being a realized desire, that will be a tree of life to them (vs 13:12).

7. If they fear the commandments of the LORD, they will have a great reward from the LORD (vs 13:13).

8. By embracing the teaching of the wise, they become a vessel of that wonderful fountain that flows from the heart of Love. To them such teaching is a spring of water that brings such refreshment and spiritual life (vs 13:14).

9. If they gain understanding, their spiritual advancement produces much grace in the lives of those who are willing to enter into it (vs 13:15).

---

[14] Noah Webster, LL.D., *An American Dictionary of the English Language*, (S. Converse:New York, 1828, republished in facsimile edition by Foundation For American Christian Education:San Francisco, 1985).

10. When the righteous ambassador exercises faithful stewardship of the Truth, he or she brings healing to many (vs 13:17).

11. If the righteous are teachable to reproof, they will always be honored. (vs13:18),

12. If another man speaks only that which is good according to the need of the moment, which edifies or gives grace to those who hear (Ephesians 4:29), there will be the blessing that good things will begin to spring up in the lives of the people around him.

13. If a man or woman keeps company with wise people, they themselves will be wise (Proverbs 13:20).

Thus, it is written: "...But the righteous will be rewarded with prosperity." (vs 13:21) This kind of prosperity goes beyond the material and touches on the immaterial things.

CHAPTER 13: TRUE PROSPERITY

True Prosperity	People, Conditions and Circumstances	A father who disciplines; a son who listens	1
		One who uses words for good	2,14
		One who guards his mouth	3
		One who is diligent	4,11
		One who acts according to truth	5
		One who is rich in the things that matter	7
		One who is righteous	9
		One who consults the proper authorities	10
		One who fears the commandment of the Lord	13
		One who has understanding and knowledge	15,16
		One who is faithful	17
		One who is teachable	18
		One who perseveres	19
		One who has wise companions	20
		One who considers the welfare of generations to come	22
	The Goal	wisdom in children	1
		fruitful discussion	2
		preserve Life	3
		enrichment in the inner man	4
		honorable behavior	5
		eternal treasures	7
		increasing hope	9
		the peace that passes comprehension	10
		increases wealth	11
		live by faith	12
		to please God	13
		to guide others	14
		to bring healing, comfort and peace	17

QUESTIONS FOR FURTHER STUDY

1. Isaiah 33: 6 says, "And He shall be the stability of your times, a wealth of salvation, wisdom, and knowledge; The fear of the Lord is his treasure." In times like we are now experiencing, in what way can we best show how we truly prosper?

2. What is the greatest treasure you have? What do you consider your greatest success?

3. Isaiah 32:17 states, "And the work of righteousness will be peace, and the service of righteousness, quietness and confidence forever." How does this show the prosperity of the righteous?

4. Isaiah 32:15, 16 shows prosperity. What is its source?

5. Consider the people, conditions and circumstances that contributed in a positive way to your greatest advancement in this world. What lessons have you learned from the people? Did you see God's hand in the circumstance? What is most meaningful to you in connection to how you prospered at that time?

"Righteousness exalts a nation, but sin is a disgrace to any people." (Proverbs 14:34)

THE GREATEST WISDOM
IN THIS LIFE

Read Proverbs 14:1—35.

> "He who walks in his uprightness fears the LORD, but he
> who is crooked in his ways despises Him." (Proverbs 14:2)

The greatest commandment is, for the Christian, the greatest wisdom for living life in this world. What is the greatest commandment?

> "And you shall love the LORD your God with all your
> heart and with all your soul and with all your might."
> (Deuteronomy 6:5)

Proverbs 14:2 helps us to understand what a person looks like who loves the LORD. The one who loves the Lord must also fear the LORD. This one will walk in uprightness before the LORD. The one who despises the LORD walks crookedly.

To walk crookedly means that you have gone off from the path of rectitude;[15] It means that a Christian who does not act, and speak with

---

[15] Rightness of principle or practice; uprightness of mind; exact conformity to truth, or to the rules prescribed for moral conduct, either by divine or human laws; (Noah Webster, LL.D., *An American Dictionary of the English Language*, (S. Converse:New York, 1828, republished in facsimile edition by Foundation For American Christian Education:San Francisco, 1985)).

regard to governing, godly, holy, spiritual and moral principles is despising the Lord that he or she claims to love.

For example, the wise woman of Proverbs 14:1 acts on the principle of building a strong home. She is called "wise," and the fear of the Lord is the beginning of wisdom (Proverbs 9:10).

1. More likely than not, this is a home wherein uprightness is practiced. It is the doing of righteousness that makes peace in the home, as Isaiah 32:17 says,

> "And the work of righteousness will be peace, and the service of righteousness, quietness and confidence forever."

2. It is a home in which love never ceases, that is, love for God, and love for one another. In as much as she fears the Lord, she obeys the Lord's commands. Therefore she loves her family.

> "For the whole Law is fulfilled in one word, in the statement, 'You shall love your neighbor as yourself.'" (Galatians 5:14).

But the foolish woman intentionally tears her own home down, and destroys her family,

"with her own hands" (Proverbs 14:1b).

The Hebrew word for hand in this case carries with it the connotation of deliberation and purpose. The foolish woman is making the choices that bring destruction in the family, and she does so knowingly. This implies that there is very little reverence toward God and very little love for her family.

On the other hand, the influence of wisdom in the heart of a godly woman is obvious:

1. She will never mock sin but strive to always have a clear conscience (vs 14:9a).
2. She will show good will toward all (vs 14:9b).

3. She will avoid bitterness and be gracious and forgiving instead (vs 14:10a).

4. Because she is upright her family will flourish (vs 14:11).

5. She will not practice that which *seems* right to men, for she understands that she must do what *is* right in the sight of God (vs 14:12).

6. She finds satisfaction and peace in doing good (vs 14:14).

7. She does not naïvely believe everything, but she researches things out before taking action (vs 14:15).

8. She is slow to anger and acts wisely in family conflicts (vs 14:17a).

9. She is crowned with knowledge because she learns what she needs to know (vs 14:18).

10. She finds great joy and honors God in being gracious to the poor (vs 14:21a, 31b).

11. She will teach the children to do good and practice kindness and truth (vs 14:22b).

12. She will speak the truth (vs14:25).

13. She will be life-giving with respect to those essential things that tend toward love, as it says,

> "The fear of the Lord is a fountain of life" (vs 14:27).

14. She will be a woman who is instructed out of God's Word, transformed by the renewing of her mind (Romans 12:2).

Thus it is the wise woman who loves the Lord, for she builds her house in uprightness. She brings principles of God into the environment, into the interactions between family members. She makes the home a place where the family finds refuge, confidence and trust. Just as it says in Proverbs 14:26:

> "In the fear of the Lord there is strong confidence, and his children will have refuge."

CHAPTER 14: THE GREATEST WISDOM IN THIS LIFE

That Which Builds, Prospers, Brings Life, and Gives Hope	**Good Behavior Shown Through the Gentleness of Wisdom**	A wise woman builds her own house	1.
		the lips of the wise preserve them	3.
		The wise considers his steps	15.
		The wise are cautious and turns away from evil	16.
		The wise are crowned with knowledge	18.
		The crown of the wise are his riches	24.
		The wise are slow to anger.	29.
		Wisdom rests in a wise man's heart.	33.
		The wise servant gains favor	35.
	The Greatest Wisdom of All	The Upright fear the Lord and love Him.	2.
		The righteous has a refuge when he dies.	32
	The Effect of a Righteous Life	Labor brings profit	4, 23
		Truth saves lives	5, 25
		Understanding is opened to the wise hearted	6.
		Among the Upright there is good will.	9.
		The wise understand the depth of the heart	10, 13
		The Upright will flourish.	11.
		A good man will be satisfied by righteousness.	14.
		The good man will be exalted.	19.
		The good man is marked by kindness and truth.	22
		The wise fear the Lord	26, 27
		There is confidence and a refuge	26
		There's a fountain of life by which deadly snares are avoided.	27

QUESTIONS FOR FURTHER STUDY

In showing love for God, one must practice uprightness. What fruit will come to those Christians who love the Lord with all their heart?

1. With regard to health? (Prov 14:30)

2. With regard to conscience? (Prov 14:9)

3. With regard to speech? (Prov 14:25)

4. With regard to essential things? (Prov 14:4)

5. With regard to expectation after death? (Prov 14:32)

"A man has joy in an apt answer, and how delightful is a timely word!" (Proverbs 15:23)

DISPOSITION AND
THE TONGUE

Read Proverbs 15:1—33.

*A Gentle answer turns away wrath, but a harsh
word stirs up anger. Proverbs 15:1*

Some of the strongest words ever written concerning the tongue and
human speech are found in the book of James. In chapter 3, the author
makes it plain that

> "no one can tame the tongue. It is a restless evil, and full
> of deadly poison," (James 3:8).

And Jesus said of the tongue that it

> "speaks out of that which fills the heart." (Matthew 12:34)

But we can control the tongue even if we can't tame it, for James wrote,

> "If anyone thinks himself to be religious and yet does not
> bridle his tongue but deceives his own heart, this man's
> religion is worthless." (James 1:26)

So we find that there is the hope of being able to bridle that which is untamable. The secret of which is found in what you allow to fill your heart. My speech is a reflection of my thoughtfulness or thoughtlessness. It is a revelation of my affections, desires or feelings. It is a manifestation of my wants, motivations, or intentions.

Thus we see in Proverbs 15 the effect that the fear of the LORD and wisdom can have on our language and communication. We are also told what to expect if we fill our hearts with folly.

If one has an attitude that is healthy toward the LORD, honoring God inwardly and honestly, the effect on his or her language can be profound. We can readily see the positive results that the fear of the Lord and wisdom have :

1. One is able to give a gentle answer that turns hostility away (vs 15:1a).
2. The wise person makes knowledge beautiful, drawing the hearts of those who hear to higher planes of understanding (vs 15:2a).
3. The wise hearted person has a healing, life-giving speech that lifts the spirit of the broken (vs 15:4a).
4. Life-giving reproof comes from the wise, and creates a heart in one who would otherwise despise his or her own soul (vs 15:5, 31–32).
5. The lips of the wise disperse knowledge, nourishing the understanding of the hearts of those who seek it (vs 15:7, 14a).
6. Those who fear the LORD in their praying speak that which is both pleasing and acceptable to God (vs 15:8b, 29b).
7. The wise one will be slow to anger and with his or her words calm controversies and allay strife (vs 15:18a).
8. By the grace given to the wise because they fear God, they are able to give timely advice that fits the need of the moment (vs 15:22–23).
9. Gracious words framing the thoughts of a pure-hearted person are pure and pleasing to the LORD (vs 15:26).
10. The speech of a wise man or woman reflects thoughtfulness in their answer. For the wise person considers how to raise the thoughts of their listeners to more lofty places than that which was previously realized by them (vs 15:28).

11. The wise person sheds such light of understanding on a subject, that there is a rejoicing and refreshing effect on those who hear (vs 15:30).

But what shall we expect if we fill our hearts with folly?

1. A foolish person creates hostility with his or her harsh words (vs 15:1b).
2. Those who do not fear the LORD dispense folly and their ugly words are offensive (vs 15:2b).
3. The words of the foolish distort the truth that eventually breaks the spirit of the hearers (vs 15:4b).
4. There is no life-giving reproof with the foolish because they despise instruction and eventually hate their own souls (vs 15:5a, 32b).
5. The hot-tempered person is foolish and does nothing but stir up anger (vs 15:18a).
6. Folly is a joy to the fool who constantly displays that he or she lacks sense by what they say (vs 15:21a).
7. The thoughts of those who do not fear the LORD prove to be disgusting and become an abhorrence to the LORD (vs 15:26a).

The beginning of knowledge and wisdom is the fear of the LORD (vs 1:7; 9:10). The fear of the LORD affects our lives in such a way that we turn away from evil, and do what is right in God's eyes. This will have a powerful impact on our actions, language and communication. The impact will be felt in our sphere of influence that is listening.

CHAPTER 15: DISPOSITION AND THE TONGUE

Disposition and the Tongue	**Positive Uses of the Tongue**	a gentle answer	vs 1
		a wise tongue	vs 2
		a soothing tongue	vs 4
		correction, reproof	vs 5, 31, 32
		wise lips	vs 7
		prayer	vs 8, 29
		intelligent mind	vs 14
		slow to anger	vs 18
		advice, instruction	vs 22, 33
		apt answer, timely word	vs 23
		pleasant words	vs 26
		righteous heart	vs 28
		a good report	vs 30
	The Effects of Positive Speech	turns away wrath, quiets contention	vs 1, 18
		makes knowledge acceptable	vs 2
		edifies the spirit (a tree of life)	vs 4
		spreads knowledge	vs 7
		seeks knowledge	vs 14
		joy, delight	vs 23
		purity	vs 26
		guidance	vs 22
		wisdom, intelligence, understanding	vs 31, 32
		nourishing effects in the body	vs 30
	Negative Uses of the Tongue	Harsh word	Vs 1
		Foolish mouth	Vs 2,14
		Perversion	Vs 4
		Foolish heart	Vs 7
		Evil plans	Vs 26
		Wicked mouth	Vs 28
	The Effects of Negative Speech	Stirs up anger	Vs 1
		Gushes forth folly	Vs 2
		Crushes the spirit	vs4
		Does not spread knowledge	Vs 7
		Feeds on folly	Vs 14
		Quenches or grieves the Spirit of God	Vs 26
		Pours forth evil things	Vs 28

QUESTIONS FOR FURTHER STUDY

Disposition is approximately equivalent to the state of mind or spirit or attitude which most often or commonly manifests itself in a person through his or her speech, choice of words and tone of voice.

1. Consider what Jesus said in Matthew 15:18-20. Explain how your speech reveals the disposition of your mind and attitude.

2. Look at Proverbs 15:1, 2, 4 and 7. What attitudes are manifested through the gentle, wise, soothing speech?

3. What disposition is seen in the harsh word? What about speech with perversion in it, what does that reveal about one's state of mind, or spirit?

4. Read Proverbs 15:26. How important is our speech with regard to our relationship with God?

5. Think about Proverbs 15:3. How much does God really see?

APPENDIX OF ANALYTICAL CHARTS

Chapter 10: Why One Should Desire to Be Righteous

Scripture	Observation	Applications	Cross-Ref
1. **The Proverbs of Solomon** A *wise* son makes a father glad. But a *foolish* son is a grief to his mother.	*Why? The wise son fears the Lord and has knowledge of the Holy One. Therefore, you can expect that the wise son will do the things that a righteous man would do. The foolish son does not listen to instruction and does not fear the Lord, therefore, you can expect that the foolish man will do what the unrighteous does.*	According to Prov 9:10, the fear of the Lord is the beginning wisdom. Thus a wise son would possess some of these traits. 1. The fear of the Lord relates to: Hating evil: thus by inference, such a person would be humble, discerning and holding to truth, and working righteousness 2. Knowledge of the Holy One relates to: an intimate relationship with the Lord and implies: understanding who He is, what His will and ways are.	Prov 9:10 Prov 15:20
2. Ill-gotten gains do not profit. but righteousness delivers from death.	Ill-gotten gains refers to the supposed profit in doing wrong. But this so called gain is in fact unprofitable because it leads to death	If you gain the whole world and lose your soul, what have you gained? Mark 8:36 But seek first His kingdom, and His righteousness; and all these things shall be added to you. Matthew 6:33	Romans 6:23 Rom 1:28-32 Romans 5:12 Rom 6:16, 21 Rom 8:6,13 Galatians 6:7, 8 1Timothy 6:9, 10
3 The Lord will not allow the righteous to hunger; but He will thrust *aside the craving of the wicked.*	There are appetites of the soul, deeper than that of the body, that only the Lord can satisfy. It is the righteous that know it..	Rather than seek a substitute for the deepest inner longings of your soul in something like food, pleasure, entertainment or sex, look only to the Lord. He alone will satisfy your hunger in your soul. He alone will quench your thirst.	Matt 5:6 John 4:14

Scripture	Observation	Applications	Cross-Ref
4. Poor is he who works with a negligent hand, but the hand of the diligent makes rich	There is a sense of deceit and fraud associated with the slack hand. There is a sense of sharpness and decisiveness and openness associated with the diligent hand. One who works with a slack hand is gripping something that is making him slack. Therefore, He cannot do the work He needs to do because his hand is full of the wrong things. A man that gets the work done is the man who does not fill his hands with false ideas, but has a clear cut vision with what to occupy his hand.	What is it that makes you slack? Do you fill your hands with things that deceive you, or are fraudulent in their promise? Thus you waste time, energy and money grasping for those things. Free hands can be employed to accomplish things that end up bearing fruit. When doing God's work, do you come with hands empty ready to bear fruit, ready to do His will, or do you come with hands filled, grasping hold of things with a false promise, things that do not belong to the matter at hand, things of self and not things of God?	Col 3:23, 24 2Tim 2:4
5. He who gathers in summer is a son who acts wisely, *but* he who sleeps in harvest is a son who acts shamefully.	When it is time to work, work. When it is time to sleep, sleep.	God's harvest is now. Discern the time. Many things are falling into place and the stage is being set for the fulfillment of prophecies concerning Christ's return. The COMING OF THE LORD IS NEAR.	Eccl 3:1-11 Eccl 3:17 Eccl 8:5, 6
6. Blessings are on the head of the righteous, but the mouth of the wicked conceals violence.	The righteous being crowned with blessings give blessings. The most outstanding characteristic of the wicked is that their mouths are overwhelmed with violence	If you are a righteous man, it never becomes a righteous man to speak as a wicked man speaks	James 3:2 Prov 10:11 Prov 26:24
7. The memory of the righteous is blessed, but the name of the wicked will rot.	*Be a righteous man, and you will leave a blessed legacy.*	Our reputation will come from our deeds. One who ends up with a good reputation was not concerned with what men thought, but rather, he dealt righteously in all his interactions with God and men.	Ps 112:6 Dan 10:11

Scripture	Observation	Applications	Cross-Ref
8. The wise of heart will receive commands, but a babbling fool will be thrown down.	This is the make up of a teachable man. *The test of a teachable man: He receives commands and therefore shows himself wise of heart.*	No one likes to hear the truth, especially when it exposes one's life. Nevertheless, we need to hear it. When a wise man speaks, we may not like it at first but I need to listen to it. The wise man may be right in his assessment!	Prov 9:8 Matt 7:24
9. He who walks in integrity walks securely, but he who perverts his ways will be found out.	*Integrity brings such stability to a life.* Perversion *makes a life unstable which eventually collapses under its own instability.*	The collapse of a life will be the thing that reveals that someone has perverted his way. The stability reveals integrity.	1Tim 5:25 Luke 6:47-49
10. He who winks the eye causes trouble, and a babbling fool will be thrown down.	*The gestures of malice of a man and the foolishness of his lips are clues to the kind of man he is. His end is that he will be thrown down.*	A jealous and envious heart, and an ambitious intent can cause you to become an enemy without cause toward the righteous man of God. Guard your heart well, for if you should become this you will surely be thrown down.	**Ps 35:19**
11. The mouth of the righteous is a fountain of life, but the mouth of the wicked conceals violence.	*One of the most important activities of the righteous person is to be able to speak the words of God correctly. He or she has to understand the needs people have at that moment.*	The kind of speech that gives life are wholesome words that edify according to the need of the moment to give grace to those who hear.	Isa 50:4 Ps 37:30 Ps 49:3 Ps101:1 Eph 4:29
12. Hatred stirs up strife, but love covers all transgressions.	If you hated someone, a transgression would be an opportunity to cause that person strife. However, if you loved, even your enemies, a transgression is an opportunity to express the love. For love covers all transgressions.	Turn transgressions from others into opportunities to show love. Cover (forgive) the transgression. After all, Jesus Christ has shed His blood for that transgression. And do not take up a reproach against your friend.	Matt 5:44 Ps 15:2, 3
13. On the lips of the discerning, wisdom is found, but a rod is for the back of him who lacks understanding	The mouth speaks from that which fills the heart. If love fills ones heart, there will be wisdom in his or her mouth. But if you lack feeling, then you will be disciplined.	*Love* abounding in real knowledge and all discernment enables one to distinguish one thing from another in such a way so as to produce the fruit of righteousness.	Rom 2:18 Phil 1:9-11

Scripture	Observation	Applications	Cross-Ref
14. Wise men store up knowledge, but with the mouth of the foolish ruin is at hand.	A wise man speaks with knowledge and people are edified, and problems are solved, but a foolish man's words bring dismay, ruin and destruction leaving people with no solution.	Words have an effect. A wise man will have the effect that brings healing, finds solutions, edifies, instructs, corrects and helps. In short, the wise man knows how to make peace. The effect of foolish speech is dismay, dissolution, destruction and ruin. No one is aided by the fool.	Prov. 9:9 Jas 3:17-18 Matt 5:9
15. The rich man's wealth is his fortress, the ruin of the poor is their poverty.	דלים dāllîm--from the root: דלל dālal--to be low, hang down. "*dal* denotes the lack of material wealth (Prov. 10:15) and social strength (Amos 2:7). Such people are contrasted with the rich (Ex 30:15; Ruth 3:10) and the great (Lev 19:5). God enjoins their protection(Ex 23:3; Lev 14:21; Isa 10:2), and promises to them justice (Isa 11:4). Only infrequently is *dal* used of spiritual poverty (cf. Jer 5:4), and in most cases such usages parallel *'ebyôn*, needy (Isa 14:30)."[16] *The rich man puts his hope in his material wealth, and the poor's hope is destroyed because he focuses on his lack. Neither one has his focus on God.*	To look at my wealth and let that be my strength, or to look at my lack and let that destroy me, both are evil. To look to the Lord no matter what the circumstance is, and be content, this is the work of God.	Phil 4:11-13
16. The wages of the righteous is life, the income of the wicked, punishment.	תבואת tebûâ't--produce, yield "The gain(te bû â)of the wicked is sin and trouble (Prov. 10:16; 15:6)"[17]	If I yield to Righteousness, that is He that is Righteous, I shall receive from Him the fruit of Life	Gal. 6:7-10 Rom 6:15-23 Rom 8:12-17

[16] *Theological Wordbook of the Old Testament, Vol I,* Leonard J. Coppes, Th.D.,(Moody Press:Chicago, 1981) p. 190.
[17] *Theological Wordbook of the Old Testament, Vol I,* Elmer A. Martins, Ph.D.,(Moody Press:Chicago, 1981) p. 95.

Scripture	Observation	Applications	Cross-Ref
	חטאת *chattâ't--sin, sin offer-ing.*[18] One reaps what he or she sows.	as my portion in this life, and in the age to come, great honor. If I yield to that evil one I shall receive only sin and corruption as my portion in this life, and in the life to come, I shall suffer a great loss!	
17. He is on the path of life who heeds instruction, but he who forsakes reproof goes astray.	A measure of where you are is: How do you listen to instruction and how do you receive reproof?	Lay aside your so-called *rights* and humble yourself. Consider and embrace the reproof whether or not you like it. That is not the issue. **The issue is to stay on the path of Life** and not to move from it but with all your might cling to that path and walk therein.	Prov. 6:23 Prov. 4:13
18. He who conceals his hatred has lying lips. and he who spreads slander is a fool.	*One who hides his intense hatred will spread slanderous lies about the one they hate.*	If there is a hint of jealousy, quickly humble yourself before you puff up against the Lord and deal falsely. This truly is folly.	Jas 3:14, 15
19. When there are many words, transgression is unavoidable, but he who restrains his lips is wise.	Talk too much and you will surely err. Be wise; say little.	*It is better to say only what is necessary.*	Ecc 5:2 Jas 3:8 Jas 1:26
20. The tongue of the righteous is as choice silver, the heart of the wicked is worth little.	The focus of this verse is on the value of that which is in the heart of both the righteous and the wicked. That which is on the tongue comes from the heart.	What is the worth of the treasure that is in your heart? Is it evil or good? Whatever it is, it will be shown by the character of your words. Not just the content, but the manner of expression.	Matt 12:33-37

---

[18] *Theological Wordbook of the Old Testament, Vol I*, G. Herbert Livingston, Ph.D., (Moody Press:Chicago, 1981) p. 277, 278.

Scripture	Observation	Applications	Cross-Ref
		So the attention needs to be focused on the character of your heart, i.e. your thoughts, affections, desires and emotions.	
21. The lips of the righteous feed many, but fools die for lack of understanding .	fools die for lack of desire."	A sure warning sign is this: If a godly man is speaking and what he is saying is feeding many, but you do not have a desire to hear it, then this is not good. This is the attitude of the fool.	Prov 1:7
22. It is the blessing of the Lord that makes rich, And He adds no sorrow to it.	This word "rich" is not necessarily speaking of material wealth, but of spiritual wealth.	How do you find wealth? Kneel before the Lord!	Matt 11:28-30
23. Doing wickedness is like sport to a fool; And so is wisdom to a man of understanding.	Why is it this way? The fool loves wickedness. The man of understanding loves the knowledge of the Holy One. Therefore, the man of understanding takes delight in wisdom. It is his diversion.	What is it that is a diversion to you? Is it wisdom? Generally, we reserve wisdom as something we seek in times of need, or in a formal setting. This is an entirely new concept, that wisdom would be the diversion of one's soul.	Prov 2:14
24. What the wicked fears will come upon him, And the desire of righteous will be granted.	מגורה **megôrâ**--*fear, terror*. The more extreme sense of fear.[19] תו täw--desire, mark. תאות--ta'äwât-- "this noun has the meaning of 'desire' extending to both good and bad objects."[20] *The Lord lets a man taste that which he loves. The wicked man will get his fill of wickedness upon his own head. The righteous man will be wholly satisfied by the Lord.*	Sometimes the desire of the righteous man may not really be that which satisfies him. For ultimately, the Lord teaches him to desire the things that satisfy eternally.	Prov 1:27 Ps 37:4 Ps 145:19 Ps 145:16 Ps 34:15-16 Ps 34:12-14 Ps 34:4

---

[19] *Theological Wordbook of the Old Testament, Vol I*, Harold G. Stigers, Ph.D., (Moody Press:Chicago, 1981) p. 157.

[20] *Theological Wordbook of the Old Testament, Vol I*, Robert L. Alden, Ph.D., (Moody Press:Chicago, 1981) p. 18.

Scripture	Observation	Applications	Cross-Ref
25. When the whirlwind passes, the wicked is no more, but the righteous has an everlasting foundation.	The wicked cannot endure the storms of life, but the righteous are not easily shaken from their foundation which is in Christ Jesus.	The question is of perseverance. Will you stick to it? Faith is crucial. Unless you believe, you cannot endure. The Lord Himself is the everlasting foundation, and He is the source of strength and the object of faith that endures.	James 1:12
26. Like vinegar to the teeth and smoke to the eyes, So is the lazy one to those who send him.	*The irritation of smoke in the eyes is just like the frustration of sending a lazy person to do an important task.*	Whatever you do, do it with all your heart.	Col 3:23
27. The fear of the Lord prolongs life, but the years of the wicked will be shortened.	The issue is one of righteousness, or turning away from evil. Sin always brings about death. *If I fear the Lord, I will generally live longer than one who is wicked.*	It is absolutely necessary for one to deny those lusts by which he or she may be tempted and to put to death those deeds which the fleshly lusts want to bring about. Otherwise, the warning to the Christian is that you will die. See Romans 8:13.	James 1:13-16
28. The hope of the righteous is gladness, but the expectation of the wicked perishes.	Given that we live in a fallen world it follows that the righteous will have trouble. It is hope that enables the righteous to have enough faith to face the trouble and walk through it. The resulting character further increases the person's hope. And in the end love for God grows deeper. There is gladness. *The hope of the righteous will be fulfilled, therefore, they will rejoice.*	God is taking us through a process that is good and finds its source in the eternal love of the Father. There is nothing He allows in one's life that first doesn't pass through His loving hands. Let us then not lose hope or faith and let us increase in love.	Romans 5:1-5

Scripture	Observation	Applications	Cross-Ref
29 The way of the Lord is a stronghold to the upright, but ruin to the workers of iniquity.	The Lord's way is a way of strength for the upright. The wicked do not understand it. The Lord's way is difficult for us because the Lord's way is supernatural essentially. It is found in the way of righteousness which springs from a spiritual, super-natural realm. The wicked find themselves in ruin for they are opposed to the Lord. It is necessary to walk in His way in order to cooperate with the Lord and to know the Lord. The wicked are ruined by what they love.	In spite of the ways of man and all the soulish opposition to the Spirit--even by the saints, who because of self interest will not enter into the Lord's way—God still accomplishes His work by His Spirit. Even the soulish saint might not understand how it happened, but usually there was one walking in uprightness before God and moving according to God's Spirit. God chooses to do mighty, faithful acts which seem impossible, through that one who finds strength in Him alone. And oh how much gets done to God's glory rather than to the glory of any man! As to the man through whom God worked, he will have that peace that passes all understanding, because he did it God's way.	James 4:4-6
30. **The righteous will never be shaken, but the wicked will not dwell in the land.**	The righteous will stand in the midst of such adversity that will destroy others who do not walk in righteousness. Those get shaken because they lack the character, the substance of the inner strength that is derived from a relationship with Him who loves righteousness. That relationship rests upon faith. The righteousness thus derived is also based on faith.	If I put my eyes on the circumstances I will be shaken. But if I put my eyes on Jesus, I shall not be moved. "God is our refuge and strength, a very present help in trouble." (Ps 46:1). The Lord is allowing the present difficulties in our lives as a test and proving of our faith. For it is absolutely essential for us to be unmovable in that which God has called us.	Phil 3:9, 10

Scripture	Observation	Applications	Cross-Ref
	Those who are convinced that God can do anything even in the midst of great difficulties, and walk in the power of the faith they have in Him, will not, indeed cannot be shaken. But the wicked will disappear.		
31. The mouth of the righteous flows with wisdom, but the perverted tongue will be cut out..	If one speaks just to impress others with his knowledge, this is not wisdom. For knowledge puffs up, and a puffed-up man is set for a great fall. A man with knowledge but no wisdom does not know how to use the knowledge correctly. A wise man takes the knowledge and uses it to help people.	This is where one should pray to God for understanding and discernment. Unless one can discern the wisdom of God, he or she can be a danger to the kingdom of God rather than an asset.	2Cor 2:6-16 James 3:17, 18
		One should not speak anything but God's wisdom with theunderstanding or discernment arising out of the illumination of God's Spirit.	
32. The lips of the righteous bring forth what is acceptable, but the mouth of the wicked, what is perverted.	There is a certain skill of speech that God teaches a man or woman who is guided by the Good Shepherd. That person will become to the Shepherd like a well-driven nail. God will use such a person to accomplish much for he or she has become a master of wisdom. *Even those who do not exercise themselves in the spiritual things of God, love to hear and find acceptable the righteous and wise answer. But no one finds the perversions of man acceptable except the perverted.*	Let there be in the present the desire to be an effective and efficient man or woman of God on point as a useful vessel to reach this generation and the discipline to be taught by the One Shepherd and the dedication to do God's will.	Ephesians 4:29 Ecc 12:11

Chapter 11: Characteristics of the Righteous and the Wicked

Scripture	Observation	Applications	Cross-Ref
1. A false balance is an abomination to the Lord, but a just weight is His delight.	*The Lord hates dishonesty in business, but delights in honesty.* God hates dishonesty in any form. A mark of Faithfulness is TRUTH. One cannot make a claim to faithfulness and remain dishonest.	*In a day and age such as ours, if you are not committed to truth, beware lest the evil one try to take advantage of you.*	Ps 101:6, 7
2. When **pride** comes, then comes dishonor, but with the humble is wisdom.	The humble hate pride and thus are wise. They will find honor.	God hates the pride of mankind, and no one who is proud will prosper in the presence of the Lord. *If you detect pride in yourself, quickly save yourself from it. Repent and go before the Lord. Cry out for deliverance. Pride is wickedness.*	Ps 101:5b James 4:6-10
3. The integrity of the upright will guide them, but the falseness of the treacherous will destroy them.	The strength and fiber of the upright will be their guide. The lack of fiber and deception of the treacherous is what destroys them	Uprightness produces a strength and substance of character that enables one to know the way to go, in good times or in desperate times, so as to avoid the way of evil.	Ps 15:2
4. Riches do not profit in the day of **wrath,** but righteousness delivers from death.	The only thing that delivers a man's life on the day of wrath is his righteousness.	There is a "day of wrath" coming. A day of God's judgment. Who will stand on that day. Material riches will not mean anything on that day. But righteousness will mean everything on that day. Do you hunger and thirst for righteousness? Do you seek first His kingdom and His righteousness?	Matt 5:6; 6:33.
5. The righteousness of the blameless will smooth his way, but the wicked will fall by his own wickedness.	Righteousness will smooth the way for the blameless, but the wickedness of the wicked is the very thing that will bring the wicked to an end.	Especially in our relationship with God, it is encouraging that being blameless and upright in God's sight will not hinder our fellowship with God.	1 John 1:6

Scripture	Observation	Applications	Cross-Ref
6. The righteousness of the upright will deliver them, but the treacherous will be caught by their own greed.	The righteousness of the upright delivers them from evil, but the greed of the treacherous will be their snare.	Beware of the greed to indulge in evil desires for your own self-gratification.	Ecc 10:8
7. When a wicked man dies, his expectation will perish, and the hope of strong men perishes.	Death is the issue. It destroys the hope of men whose hope is in this life. It ruins the expectation of men whose eyes were fixed on this life. It is a trap--a grievous trap-- to have one's hope in this life alone.	*"O death, where is your victory? O death, where is your sting?"* (1Corinthians 15:55) It is not wise to put your expectation of good in a system run by the evil one. You must be on your guard. Remember what you are: You are a citizen of the kingdom of Jesus Christ. Let all your hope and expectations for good be firmly directed toward and thoroughly rooted in the kingdom of our Lord Jesus Christ. There is an everlasting hope for those who believe in the Lord Jesus Christ.	Matt 6:19-21.
8. The righteous is delivered from trouble, but the wicked takes his place.	**2502** חלץ--**châlats,** *khaw-lats:* a prim. root; *to pull* off; hence (intens.) to strip, (reflex) to depart; by impl. to deliver, equip (for fight); present, strengthen;: --arm (self), (go, ready) armed (x man, soldier), deliver, draw out, make fat, loose, (ready) prepared, put off, take away, withdraw self. [21]	Because of righteousness the man is pulled off from the trouble. But the wicked man enters into the righteous man's place. Haman and Mordecai illustrate this.	Esther 7:10

---

[21] James Strong, S.T.D., LL.D., _The New Strong's Complete Dictionary of Bible Words_, introduction by John R Kohlenberger, III, (Thomas Nelson Publishers:Atlanta, London,Vancouver, 1996) p. 368.

Scripture	Observation	Applications	Cross-Ref
9. With his mouth the godless man destroys his neighbor, but through knowledge the righteous will be delivered.	**2611** חנף—**chânêph**, *khaw-nafé'*; **from** 2610; soiled (i.e. with sin), impious:-- hypocrite, (-ical). [22] The kind of knowledge here is the contemplative perception of the wise man who hears, observes and understands the godless, and knows what they are saying and doing. He will be delivered.	The "godless" in the Hebrew is the 'hypocrite'. A Christian could be a hypocrite, he or she could be soiled with sin, or impious, and destroy his neighbor with his mouth. Do not be deceived.	James 4:11, 12
10. When it goes well with the righteous, the city rejoices, And when the wicked perish there is glad shouting.	There seems to be something in mankind that intuitively understands the difference between the righteous and the wicked so that when righteousness prevails, people rejoice.	A city rejoicing when things go well with the righteous is indicative of love, for love rejoices with the truth. But what will happen when lawlessness abounds? (Matthew 24:12)	James 3:13-14 1Cor 13:6
11. By the blessing of the upright a city is exalted, but by the mouth of the wicked it is torn down.	The word "blessing" is the same word in Proverbs 10:22. The statement tells us that the mouth of the wicked can tear down the blessing and prosperity brought to it by the upright.	The treasure of wisdom and knowledge possessed by the upright is such that it exalts, in a good way, a city. The media has the power to tear down the blessing and prosperity of a city or build it up.	
12 He who despises his neighbor lacks sense, but a man of understanding keeps silent.	One who tells on his neighbor is one who despises him, but the one who has knowledge of the Holy One will remain silent.	All men fall short. Love covers a multitude of sins. Pray for your neighbor and plead with God for him for mercy and repentance.	Gen 18:22-33
13 He who goes about as a talebearer reveals secrets, But he who is trustworthy conceals a matter.	The "faithful of spirit" is one who is reliable or faithful and thus can be trusted with crucial, personal and private information.	To be a talebearer is a terrible thing to do. It always causes divisions among God's people. Some things must not be told to others.	Leviticus 19:16

---

[22] Ibid. p. 371.

127

Scripture	Observation	Applications	Cross-Ref
14 Where there is no guidance the people fall, but in abundance of counselors there is victory.	Leadership is important. *People need leadership or else they fall.* People need guidance. There is safety in speaking with people who know and have expertise in a certain field.	There is a time and a place where men are sought out for counsel, and there is a time where only One is sought, and He alone can give the answer.	Prov 15:22; 16:1; 19:21; 20:18; 24:6.
15 He who is surety for a stranger will surely suffer for it, but he who hates going surety is safe.	**A money principle**. Do not cosign for a loan with someone you do not know well. And if you hate doing it you are safe.	Be responsible and pay what you owe. The stranger will not care so much that he did not pay the loan, and it will not bother him that you had to pay instead. But if you know the one who cosigned for your loan, you will want to repay what you borrowed.	Prov 6:1-5; 27:13
16. A gracious woman attains honor, and violent men attain riches.	**There is a cause and effect.** The graciousness of a gracious woman is the cause. The effect is that she will obtain honor. The violence of sinful men is the cause. The effect is they obtain riches by force but they will not attain honor. Money is not better than honor. Those who choose money over honor corrupt themselves.	Every action, and attitude--every choice made by man will cause something to happen, or will set in motion a chain of events that results in a predictable end. We all must give account to God in the end.	Prov 31:28, 30
17 The merciful man does himself good, but the cruel man does himself harm.	**One reaps what he or she sows.** A merciful man does himself good because he will receive mercy. The cruel man damages his own soul as his heart is hardened to other people's pain. The cruel man no one likes and he will eventually be treated with the same cruelty by which he has made others suffer.	If you want to be loved, love. If you want to be shown mercy, then show mercy. How you treat others is how you shall be treated.	Matt 5:7; Matt 25:34--46

Scripture	Observation	Applications	Cross-Ref
18 The wicked earns deceptive wages, but he who sows righteousness gets a true reward.	**Things do not appear as they really are.** The wages of the wicked are deceptive. They cannot be taken with you when you die. This is what makes them deceptive. The righteous man has his reward stored up in heaven. This is a true reward.	The devil will bless you with success in this world if you are willing to compromise (Matt 4:8, 9). Does that mean that it is the devil that is blessing you if you are a "success" in this world? No, God may bless His people with abundance also in this life. (Job 42:12) But the righteous man understands that his true reward is not in this life but in the life to come.	Galatians 6:8, 9James 3:18
19 He who is steadfast in righteousness will attain to life, and he who pursues evil will bring about his own death.	The man who pursues righteousness will attain to life. The man who pursues evil is responsible for his own death.	Life and Death are set before us. If we choose life, then we must choose righteousness. If we choose evil, then we are choosing death.	Rom 8:13
20 The perverse in heart are an abomination to the Lord, but the blameless in their walk are His delight.	The Lord hates perversities in our hearts. The Lord is pleased when we walk blamelessly	We cannot stand in our own righteousness, but rather in that which comes from God on the basis of faith. For without faith it is impossible to please Him.	Prov 13:6 Ps 1:1-3 Ps 119:1-8
21. Assuredly the evil man will not go unpunished, but the descendants of the righteous will be delivered.	There is no question about it. If a man walks in righteousness, he will find that God will bless even his children and their children. But the evil man leaves no stable heritage for his children nor his grandchildren.	The heritage a man leaves for his family is extraordinarily important, especially in this world.	Isaiah 33:5, 6 Ps 37:23-34
22 As a ring of gold in a swine's snout, so is a beautiful woman who lacks discretion.	Outward beauty is marred by a lack of inward discretion.	It is the inward qualities that really make a woman beautiful. Far greater in value are the inner qualities than the outward qualities that the world so emphasizes.	1Pet 3:1-6

Scripture	Observation	Applications	Cross-Ref
23 The desire of the righteous is only good, but the expectation of the wicked is wrath.	A righteous man desires good and his expectation is salvation. The wicked man desires evil, and his expectation is wrath.	Count yourself as being dead to evil desires.	Colossians 3:5
24 There is one who scatters, yet increases all the more, and there is one who withholds what is justly due, but it results only in want.	Giving liberally to the poor results in blessing from the Lord of increased resources to continue the liberality.. But the one who is unwilling to give justly to help the poor, that one will suffer want.	There are many needs all around. Our resources are: 1 Time 2 Money 3 Strength Pray on how to use your resources.	James 2:5
25 The generous man will be prosperous, and he who waters will himself be watered.	Watering the lives of people with the things of God will make one even wealthier in those things, for God adds His treasure to you.	Do not become stingy with the things God has given you, but ask for wisdom and insight on what to give, when and to whom.	Prov 3:9, 10 2Cor 9:6, 7
26 He who withholds grain, the people will curse him, but blessingwill be on the head of him who sells it.	Blessings come with the one who does what is right when it is time. Men have a sense of justice within them being made in the image of God. Therefore, aman who does not do right can expect to be hated.	Do what is right and you will be blessed.	Prov 24:24
27 He who diligently seeks good seeks favor, but he who searches after evil, it will come to him.	**A man will find that which he seeks.** God's unmerited favor is given to those who in their heart seek good. Evil will come to the one who is seeking her.	Those who seek good must seek God and wait upon Him. Then they will find favor from Him as they trust in His Son. There is no good apart from God. The Lord promises all those who seek Him with all their hearts that He will let them find him.	Esther 7:10
28 He who trusts in his riches will fall but the righteous will flourish like the green leaf.	The issue is : Do you trust God or money?	The one trusting in money may lose it all in a short period of time. God may have to remove it. But the one trusting in God has true stability even in the midst of economic disaster.	Matt 6:24

Scripture	Observation	Applications	Cross-Ref
29 He who troubles his own house will inherit wind, and the foolish will be servant to the wise-hearted.	To say 'trouble one's house' in this sense most likely means to cause trouble for those who are your family, or those with whom you live. To say that he will inherit wind implies that such a one will wind up without anything. This one's folly is born in self-centeredness, for very little consideration is given to the rest of the household.	Unless a person learns to deny himself and take up the cross daily, that person is in danger of losing all he or she has.	Proverbs 15:27
30 The fruit of the righteous is a tree of life, and he who is wise wins souls.	What flows from the heart of the righteous gives life to others, and wins the hearts and minds of men and women for the Lord.	It is for the Christian to allow the fruit of the Spirit to come forth, so that as Jesus said, "rivers of living water," (John 7:38) might flow from within, unhindered by the outward man, and impart life to others.	John 7:38
31 If the righteous will be rewarded in the earth, How much more the wicked and the sinner!	God is not partial in judgment. Both the righteous and the wicked will be rewarded in this life, and stand before his throne and give account for the deeds done in the body.	"Therefore also we have as our ambition, whether at home or absent, to be pleasing to Him." (2 Corinthians 5:9).	2Cor 5:10 2Cor 5:9-15

Chapter 12: Counseling –A Painstaking Labor of Love

Scripture	Observation	Applications	Cross-Ref
1 Whoever loves discipline loves knowledge, but he who hates reproof is stupid.	It means that when someone comes to bring reproof, do not dismiss it but take it to heart and evaluate it carefully and learn from it.	See godly discipline as coming from the Lord. Accept it no matter how hard it is. Recognize the purpose of it. And apply its lesson toward that purpose, recognizing that righteousness is the end product.	Heb 12:11
2 A good man will obtain favor from the Lord, but He will condemn a man who devises evil.	God shows kindness, grace, and acceptance to the morally good person.	In as much as grace and truth were realized through Jesus Christ, He is the only one who could have brought mankind into this grace in which we now stand by faith in the Lord Jesus.	John 1:17 Prov 3:3, 4
3 A man will not be established by wickedness, but the root of the righteous will not be moved.	The righteous man will not be quickly moved away from righteousness, and when the test comes, he withstands the opponent and is victorious.	Realize that it is the *root* where the strength of my life will be established. I must have my roots first in Christ and in a practical way, I cannot move away from His Word.	Jude 12 Prov 10:25 Matt 7:24-27
4 An excellent wife is the crown of her husband, but she who shames him is as rottenness in his bones.	An excellent wife will make a man feel like a king	She will become that which distinguishes her husband among men as one who has something of priceless value.	Prov 31:11 Prov 31:10. Eph 5:25-33.
5 The thoughts of the righteous are just, but the counsels of the wicked are deceitful.	The righteous person's thoughts are based on fact and are reasonable.	In giving counsel, it is absolutely necessary to understand the facts, and use sound reasoning, based on that which is true and morally right. Anything else is *deceitful* and *wicked*. God cares about the counsel one gives.	Job 42:7

Scripture	Observation	Applications	Cross-Ref
6 The words of the wicked lie in wait for blood, but the mouth of the upright will deliver them.	While unrighteous men try to ambush the righteous with their words, righteous speech overthrows their wicked words which were intended to destroy.	Pray for the power to speak righteously and the courage to speak it and the wisdom to know the right timing.	Prov 1:11, 16, 18
7 The wicked are overthrown and are no more but the house of the righteous will stand.	The righteous have a sure foundation. God will overthrow their enemies.	Be faithful to the God of your righteousness. Trust Him to act in your defense.	Prov 10:25
8 A man will be praised according to his insight, but one of perverse mind will be despised.	Men recognize excellent insight and will tell it to others when they hear it. If your insight is excellent, it can do nothing but bring honor to God.	If you speak with excellence, bringing sound words and wisdom in your speech, it will be noted among men. Nevertheless, this is not the motive for speaking sound words and using insight in counsel. The motive must be to serve mankind in ministry to their needs, to exalt righteousness, and glorify God by doing His will.	Acts 4:13
9 Better is he who is lightly esteemed and has a servant, than he who honors himself and lacks bread.	Humility is always better than pride.	The one to pattern our lives after is the One who walked lowly, as Jesus did.	John 5:31
10 A righteous man has regard for the life of his beast, but the compassion of the wicked is cruel.	The righteousness of the righteous man teaches him to show compassion even for a beast.	If a righteous man has compassion on a beast, how much more so should he show compassion toward those who are made in the image of God?	Deut 25:4
11 He who tills his land will have plenty of bread but he who pursues vain things lacks sense.	If you use your time to do the important things, you will not be lacking, but to pursue empty things is quite foolish--a waste of time and energy.	Our lives are too short to waste precious time on things that are vain.	2Thess 3:10

Scripture	Observation	Applications	Cross-Ref
12 The wicked desires the booty of evil men, but the root of the righteous yields fruit.	This verse seems to mean that the wicked are full of covetousness towards other men's income, and the righteous not only earn their own income, but give out of their earnings to meet the needs of others.	Rather than covet the things others have, earn your own living and give from what you have to contribute to the people in need.	2Cor 9:7
13 An evil man is ensnared by the transgression of his lips, but the righteous will escape from trouble.	One's words will either save you from trouble, or deliver you into a trap for which there is no escape.	I cannot be careless in my speech and expect that I will not encounter trouble.	James 3:2
14 A man will be satisfied with good by the fruit of his words, and the deeds of a man's hands will return to him.	The speech of man is powerful. What a man speaks may have the effect that satisfies the soul. The right word spoken can accomplish much good. The good or evil that a man does will come back to him.	Often we do not consider the power of the spoken word. It increases as one increases in influence. It is not acceptable for a spiritual man who is a leader to speak inappropriately.	Eph 4:29 James 1:26.
15 The way of a fool is right in his own eyes, but a wise man is he who listens to counsel.	Other people see things in your life that you do not necessarily see. Therefore, if someone is willing to risk telling you what they see, it is important enough to listen to them because they may be right.	A wise man never forgets how to listen. Many godly men are around and they recognize that things may elude our understanding, and it is good to listen to it, evaluate it, and pray.	1Thess 5:20, 21
16 A fool's vexation is known at once, but a prudent man conceals dishonor.	A man lacking in self-control is the one who instantly expresses his annoyance about someone or something. But self-control in speech will keep you from having to withdraw your foot from your mouth.	It is important to carefully consider this: **if** it does not edify, if there is not a need to know, then do not speak it to anyone. Always bring those things that could be called a vexation to the throne of God.	Phil 4:6, 7
17 He who speaks truth tells what is right, but a false witness, deceit.	The one who speaks truth tells things the way they are with objectivity and clear evidence giving an accurate picture so that one can take the appropriate action.	The truth is important. It brings about decisions and choices. There is no substitute for the truth.	James 3:17

Scripture	Observation	Applications	Cross-Ref
18 There is one who speaks rashly like the thrusts of a sword, but the tongue of the wise brings healing.	Some men do not realize that they wound people with their words. They do not understand that they spoke hastily, and are not sensitive to how other people take their words. Someone who knows people and is wise enough to shed light on the behavior of all types of personalities can help both the one speaking rashly, and the ones being wounded.	A wise person should understand mankind so that he or she can become effective and have the wisdom to help people in their condition.	1Cor 3:10
19 Truthful lips will be established forever, but a lying tongue is only for a moment.	God will honor truthful lips, and the honor will be eternal. No one will remember the lie which was told to gain something temporary, but the effect of truthful lips is eternal.	To know and acknowledge the truth is one thing. To love the truth is another. By the love of the truth, one can avoid going into willful deception.	Eph 4:25
20 Deceit is in the heart of those who devise evil, but counselors of peace have joy.	Deception comes before evil schemes. And Deception is used to carry out the schemes. Joy comes to the counselors of peace because by their truthful counsel, people are set free from the evil schemes and scams.	What kind of counselor are you? Is your counsel faithful to the truth, and by it, do you help people to turn from evil?	Isa 50:4
21 No harm befalls the righteous, but the wicked are filled with trouble.	Those who have made the Lord their refuge, He will be a shield to them. Nothing will harm them. Only that which God allows for our testing and for our ultimate good will enter our lives, and the evil one cannot do anything apart from the permission of the Lord.	Walking by faith and making the Lord your refuge is the safest place to be in this life.	Ps 91:9, 10
22 Lying lips are an abomination to the Lord, but those who deal faithfully are His delight.	God despises lying lips. God rejoices greatly in those who deal faithfully.	Those who fear the Lord will turn away from lying lips and deal faithfully.	Psalm 101:6,7

Scripture	Observation	Applications	Cross-Ref
23 A prudent man conceals knowledge, but the heart of fools proclaims folly.	Knowledge is something to conceal and only to be revealed at the right time to the right people if ever at all.	It is not necessary to speak to people to prove that you know. Such is really pride and the opposite of prudence. It is equal to trying to get men's approval. It is evil. Don't do it.	Prov 10:14
24 The hand of the diligent will rule, but the slack hand will be put to forced labor.	Those who are responsible will be given responsibility, those who are not responsible, will lose their liberties and be forced to bear some responsibility	Those who put forth a diligent effort in the Lord's work will be given much responsibility. Do not be slack about the things that really matter.	1Cor 4:1, 2
25 Anxiety in the heart of man weighs it down, but a good word makes it glad.	People carry heavy burdens these days and need to hear a good word to cheer them up.	It is important to encourage people according to what they are facing with words that shed light and give hope.	Matthew 11:28
26 The righteous is a guide to his neighbor, but the way of the wicked leads them astray.	Our neighbors watch the way we live. if we are living according to righteousness we will be a guide to them. If we are living unrighteously, we will lead them astray.	Set an example, let your light shine in such a manner that your neighbors, if they follow your example, will glorify God.	Matthew 5:16
27 A slothful man does not roast his prey, but the precious possession of a man is diligence.	Diligence has its rewards and its effects. The lazy man does not know it because he is not willing to do the required work. But diligence is a precious possession.	Apply diligence to spiritual matters, Especially prayer and meditation.	Ps 1:2
28 In the way of righteousness is life, and in its pathway there is no death.	The Path of Righteousness is not religion. It is the path of Faith. Not faith in faith, but faith in Christ Jesus the Lord. And faith is being fully persuaded in your heart that what God said about His Son is true.	Be grateful that eternal life has been revealed through faith in the Lord Jesus Christ. And along with this comes the righteousness from God on the basis of faith. Eternal life is not based on our own righteousness, and there is nothing we can do to merit it.	Rom 5:1

Scripture	Observation	Applications	Cross-Ref
		Christ has done it all. This is what we believe, and God counts us righteous because we believe..	

Chapter 13: True Prosperity

Scripture	Observation	Applications	Cross-Ref
1 A wise son accepts his father's discipline, but a scoffer does not listen to rebuke.	The wise son has gone two steps beyond the foolish one. First he listened and then he accepted it.	Do not be in the scoffer's shoes. For the scoffer does not even give the Lord a chance to be heard, for he will not listen to Him.	Ps 1:1
2 From the fruit of a man's mouth he enjoys good, but the desire of the treacherous is violence.	Since a man speaks out of that which fills his heart, a man who fills his heart with good, will enjoy the fruit of that which is good, but this man must desire good to speak good.	What is it that is in your heart, good or treachery? You will reap what your desires dictate.	Matt 12:35
3 The one who guards his mouth preserves his life. The one who opens wide his mouth comes to ruin.	It is better to not speak too quickly, but guard your heart, much damage can come from it.	It is more important than you think, be careful how you speak. What you say may be your undoing.	James 1:19
4 The soul of the sluggard craves and gets nothing, but the soul of the diligent is made fat.	The diligent will prosper. The sluggard has cravings, but is empty handed. You must do more than just crave something. Desire is a function of the soul but so is the will, the power to choose and act. A person has to engage his or her will to become diligent. The word *craves* suggests that the craving is a physical appetite. The fact that this person is called a sluggard suggests that there is no desire in the soul, only craving in the body.	Getting things done: 1) **Desire** it. 2) **Define** the requirements. 3) **Develop** a strategy. 4) **Decide** to do it. 5) **Discipline** yourself to do it.	
5 A righteous man hates falsehood, but a wicked man acts disgustingly and shamefully.	The correlation is between falsehood and disgusting, shameful behavior. The wicked, being deceived, does not really understand how disgusting and shameful his or her behavior is.	There is nothing shameful and disgusting about TRUTH. Love the truth and live in truth and you will not have a reason to be ashamed.	Col 3:9

Scripture	Observation	Applications	Cross-Ref
6 Righteousness guards the one whose way is blameless, but wickedness subverts the sinner.	A blameless man cannot be ruined, his righteousness guards his life.	Do you want to walk without stumbling? Then, you must take seriously to heart the absolute necessity to walk in righteousness as it applies to all areas of your life.	Ps 15:5
7 There is one who pretends to be rich and has nothing. Another pretends to be poor, but has great wealth.	The former is rich in the wrong things. In the things pertaining to God and eternal life, he or she is empty. The latter is rich towards God, but in the things of this world he or she is deemed poor.	There are many eternal things. Whatever those things are, they are priceless. No amount of money can buy these things. They are not obtained with the things of this world, but are obtained through diligently supplementing your faith in order to complete and perfect it, in order to fill what is lacking, and in order to expand it, supplement it with moral excellence, knowledge, self-control, perseverance, godliness, brotherly kindness, and love . Pursue eternal things.	Matt 6:19 2Pet 1:4—7
8 The ransom of a man's life is his riches, but the poor hears no rebuke.	Because a man is rich, he is more likely to be sued with exaggerated charges, but no one wants to sue the poor man because he is poor.	True justice is not affected by greed.	1Tim 6:10
9 The light of the righteous rejoices, but the lamp of the wicked goes out.	The righteous life shines brightly(with hope, purpose and meaning), the wicked life is dark and leads to utter darkness.	We are called the children of light, and therefore are exhorted to walk as children of light. Who we are should determine how we walk.	Matt 5:16 Eph 5:8-14 John 1:4
10 Through presumption comes nothing but strife, but with those who receive counsel is wisdom.	To do something without authority or permission will lead to strife. Seek godly counsel.	Never presume upon God. How can this be prevented? Never do anything without first seeking God's permission, authority and guidance.	John 5:30 John 5:19

Scripture	Observation	Applications	Cross-Ref
11 Wealth obtained by fraud dwindles, but the one who gathers by labor increases it.	honest work(that which comes by labor)increases wealth (income and character).	Fraud kills character. You must be honest in all your dealings. **The income of a man's work is not just money.** The most important thing is the character that God builds in one's life through his or her work. Remember that it is Jesus that you serve on the earth.	Col 3:23, 24
12 Hope deferred makes the heart sick, but desire fulfilled is a tree of life.	When a person's hope is realized, that one is able to go on in faith and love, but unrealized hope causes people to lose their will to live.	Our hope in Christ is a sure thing based upon the promise of God. Never lose sight of your hope no matter what the circumstances of your life turns out to be, your hope remains because of God's promise.	Rom 5:5
13 The one who despises the word will be in debt to it, but the one who fears the commandment will be rewarded.	How important is the Word of God! We will answer to it or be rewarded by it.	Listen to God and His Word.	Ps 19:11
14 The teaching of the wise is a fountain of life, to turn aside from the snares of death.	Wise men's teachings will save you from deadly traps of evil and sin.	Do you know a wise man? Then you will become wise to listen to him. What he tells you is meant to save you from death.	Prov 14:27 Prov 10:11
15 Good understanding produces favor, but the way of the treacherous is hard.	From the parallelism of this passage it can be inferred that a person who is treacherous does not have a good understanding, and therefore, has come to the wrong conclusions affecting their loyalty to a particular relationship. It then becomes very hard to find favor in that relationship.	If you are treacherous your life will be hazardous. Let faithfulness be the mark of your life.	Lk 16:24 *ibid.*

Scripture	Observation	Applications	Cross-Ref
16 Every prudent man acts with knowledge, but a fool displays folly.	Wisdom is not only having the correct information, but understanding it and using it according to discernment's dictates.	How do others perceive you, a man of prudence or of folly? It is what you do that tells which one you are to others.	Prov 12:23
17 A wicked messenger falls into adversity, but a faithful envoy brings healing.	No one likes an untrustworthy messenger because he or she cannot convey the message faithfully and that turns everything into turmoil.	Spiritual warfare comes through unfaithfulness in conveying the messages entrusted to one's charge. Be faithful with what you are given.	Prov 25:13
18 Poverty and shame will come to him who neglects discipline, but he who regards reproof will be honored.	Listen to what you are told when you are being reproved, then you will find honor.	A man in a pit has a hard time getting out without someone else's hand reaching in to save him. Think of reproof that way, and realize that if you are reproved someone is trying to save you from the pit.	Prov 15:5
19 Desire realized is sweet to the soul, but it is an abomination to fools to dep art from evil.	The evil man only has evil desires. That is why he is evil. In his soul evil is his sweet satisfaction, but not so with the righteous.	The desire in a man is a strong force--the satisfaction of which drives men into actions that are evil. A Christian is to count himself as dead to evil desires which embodies one of the facets of idolatry.	Col 3:1-5 Ps 37:1-7
20 He who walks with wise men will be wise but the companion of fools will suffer harm.	You will be like the ones you hang out with.	If there are wise men in your life, it will be a good thing to listen to them	Prov 15:31
21 Adversity pursues sinners, but the righteous will be rewarded with prosperity	The goal with the righteous is to please God and attain to righteousness through faith and the fear of the Lord.	May the Lord prosper your way in the pursuit of Him. That the people, conditions, and circumstances may be a positive force to bring about Christ-likeness in your life.	Ps 32:10

Scripture	Observation	Applications	Cross-Ref
22 A good man leaves an inheritance to his children's children, and the wealth of the sinner is stored up for the righteous.	A good man impacts not only his generation, but his children and grandchildren. A man's legacy should have positive results even to the third generation.	What kind of inheritance will your grandchildren have? Leave them with priceless spiritual treasures that will sustain them in their evil generation.	Ps 37:25
23 Abundant food is in the fallow ground of the poor, but it is swept away by injustice.	This abundance is unrealized potential, for the poor man was unjustly kept from planting.	Often the poor are not able to realize the potential abundance in his life because of the evil of injustice that keeps him down.	James 2:6.
24 He who spares his rod hates his son, but he who loves him, disciplines him diligently	The rod is effective in driving out foolishness.	Consider that discipline not only refers to the rod, but it also refers to instruction. Do not forget one's obligation to teach your sons and daughters through the discipline of instruction.	Hebrews 12:7
25 The righteous has enough to satisfy his appetite, but the stomach of the wicked is in want.	The righteous are amply supplied and are satisfied.	God faithfully supplies those who fear Him.	Ps 145:19

Chapter 14: Wisdom and Folly

Scripture	Observation	Applications	Cross-Ref
1 The wise woman builds her house, but the foolish tears it down with her own hands	The idea here is that she (the wise woman) builds her family rather than the house that the family lives in. The foolish woman destroys her family. The idea is that she is doing it with deliberation and purpose.	This is the kind of woman that intentionally destroys the family. She is foolish for this reason, and what she does is evil.	Ruth 4:11
2 He who walks in his uprightness fears the Lord, but he who is crooked in his ways despises Him.	This one who despises the Lord has deliberately chosen a crooked path in which evil is generally the common practice. The evil way is marked by lust of the flesh, lust of the eyes, and the pride of life. A person who chooses a crooked path cannot love the Lord.	Jesus told us that if one keeps His commandments, then it is he that loves Him. To love the Lord is to also fear Him. (reverently respect Him as well as be afraid of His judgment if you do evil.)	John 14:21 1John 2:15, 16
3 In the mouth of the foolish is a rod for his back; But the lips of the wise will preserve them. .	The idea is that in the speech of a fool you will find the words that can be used to discipline and rebuke him. The language of the wise will guard them, but the words of the foolish will expose them as fools	For by your words you shall be justified, and by your words you shall be condemned.	Matt 12:37
4 Where no oxen are, the manger is clean,[1249] But much increase comes by the strength of the ox.	Where there are life's activities, there are signs of life left behind. Where life's activities have ceased, there are signs of a museum.	There are some essential things and some non-essential things. Never destroy the essential in favor of the non-essential. It is non-essential to have a clean manger, but quite imperative to have a good and healthy ox to produce a crop, and work the land.	

Scripture	Observation	Applications	Cross-Ref
5 A faithful witness will not lie, But a false witness speaks lies.	One is a truth witness. One is a sham witness. A truth witness gives true testimony because they see the truth. The sham witness cannot recognize the truth. Truth means nothing to him, and so he testifies deceitfully	What is your perspective on life? Can you see the truth of what is happening around you? Ask God to give you the ability to perceive the truth, that when you testify, your testimony will be clear with respect to the facts, and your testimony will be true.	Rev 1:5; 3:14
6 A scoffer seeks wisdom and finds none, But knowledge is easy to him who has understanding.	A scoffer is a fool. They seek wisdom and do not find it because they do not seek after the Personal God. They do not welcome the things of God and they hate instruction.	If you want wisdom, do not be a scoffer.	
7 Leave the presence of a fool, or you will not discern words of knowledge.	The language of a fool does not contain knowledge.	The best thing to do is leave the presence of such a person.	Proverbs 23:9
8 The wisdom of the prudent is to understand his way, But the folly of fools is deceit.	It is prudent to learn who you are and why you do what you do. It is deception to refuse to learn this, and to deny it.	If you know who you are, then you will be able to discern the difference between your natural self and that which is of the Spirit of God.	1Cor. 3:19-20.
9 Fools mock at sin. But among the upright there is good will.	A fool when he is caught and shown his own guilt just mocks the sin and the guilt. Remember the fool despises wisdom and instruction. In short he goes into deception. That is why he mocks the truth.	When confronted with sin, humble yourself and repent.	Prov. 3:34
10 The heart knows its own bitterness, and a stranger does not share its joy.	It takes wisdom to draw out people's heart. It takes love to share in it.	Lord, grant me wisdom to detect the suffering heart and love to share in their lives.	Job 21:25.

Scripture	Observation	Applications	Cross-Ref
11 The house of the wicked will be destroyed, but the tent of the upright will flourish..	The house which seems more permanent than a tent gets destroyed because it is the house of the wicked. What appears at first to be the least becomes that which flourishes because it is of God, for God supports the upright.	Maintain uprightness, then you will eventually flourish, especially your family.	Prov. 14:34.
12 There is a way which seems right to a man, but its end is the way of death.	Man's way ends in death. He thought it seemed right, but man's way is far below God's.	Sin is what brings forth death. Even a man's mind is fallen. So a man cannot with his mind alone find the path of life. Let me learn God's ways. They are much higher than man and always lead to life.	Prov. 12:15. Prov. 16:25.
13 Even in laughter the heart may be in pain, and the end of joy may be grief.	Men have the capacity to hide what is going on in their hearts and try to disguise it with outward appearances.	It requires that a man of God be discerning and sensitive to see the truth in a person. May God grant me to see what is below the surface to find the truth.	Eccl. 2:1,2.
14 The backslider in heart will have his fill of his own ways, but a good man will be satisfied with his.	If a man chooses to live for self and live in sin, he will eventually have his fill and find the resulting emptiness. But the good man is satisfied because he finds fullness of life within himself coming from God's Holy Spirit.	One man is living for the gratification of the flesh which is always temporary and leads to spiritual destitution. The other man seeks that which satisfies spiritually and finds eternal treasures which also satisfy his soul.	Prov. 1:31
15 The naive believes everything, but the prudent man considers his steps.	It is important that you do not trust the words of men. They are deceitful, and many smooth talkers take advantage of people who want to do good, but in their gullibility believe the scam.	Learn to consider the steps of your feet, and watch out for your own motives, lest they betray you.	

Scripture	Observation	Applications	Cross-Ref
16 A wise man is cautious and turns away from evil, but a fool is arrogant and careless	This foolish man's carelessness will eventually destroy him. The wise man's caution will save him.	It is pure arrogance to ignore the evidence and the preponderance of counsel that points in a singular direction to avoid an evil. If you go forward toward evil, then the consequences are yours to own. The motive of the heart is revealed by what a man chooses to do.	Ps 34:14
17 A quick-tempered man acts foolishly, and a man of evil devices is hated.	Because he is quick-tempered, he does not do righteously but acts according to unrighteousness.	Let me learn to be ready to hear, slow to respond, slow to anger.	James 1:20.
18 The naive inherit folly, the prudent are crowned with knowledge.	The person who cultivates prudence will receive a great honor, that is, knowledge. The one who cultivates naivety will receive folly.	You get what you cultivate. The prudent never reap folly, only knowledge. The naive never reap knowledge, only folly. What do you cultivate?	
19 The evil will bow down before the good, and the wicked at the gates of the righteous.	The righteous will judge the evil.	The Lord is righteous, and His righteousness will fill the earth, and evil will be judged.	Prov. 11:29.
20 The poor are hated even by his neighbor, but those who love the rich are many.	What is really meant by this is that men love money.	Are you motivated by the love of money? Flee such a thing. There is a great evil in the love of money.	1Tim. 6:10
21 He who despises his neighbor sins, but happy is he who is gracious to the poor.	Real happiness is not found in money, but seeing the value of a poor man's soul and showing grace to him freely this pleases God.	Can you see the value of a man's soul? Can you treat a man with grace?	
22 Will they not go astray who devise evil? But kindness and truth will be to those who devise good.	Those who think up evil things will go off the path of kindness and truth. Those who think up good things will know kindness and truth.	Kindness and truth are eternal treasures by which one lives on the earth in a way pleasing to God. May the Lord instruct me in this way.	John 1:17

Scripture	Observation	Applications	Cross-Ref
23 In all labor there is profit, but mere talk leads only to poverty. It's not what you say, but what you do that counts.	All labor is inclusive of any field of work, and the profit is the fruit of the labor. A man reaps what he sows. Just talking about getting something done does not actually get the thing done. Success comes from applying effort to the task in such a way so as to bear the fruit.	The fruit of the Lord which He would have us bear, is found in everything our hand is applied to do, if it is applied with a whole heart.	Colossians 3:23, 24.
24 The crown of the wise is their riches, butthe folly of fools is foolishness.	**The riches of the wise are** more than money. It is a great spiritual treasure that comes from the fear of the Lord and walking with Him.	Jesus taught us to pursue the true riches, and to be rich towards God.	Prov. 10:22
25 A truthful witness saves lives[5315], But he who speaks lies is treacherous.	**5315 נפש nephesh;** *neh'-fesh;* from 5314; prop. a breathing creature, i.e. animal or (abstr.) vitality: used very widely in a lit., accommodated or fig. sense(bodily or mental):--any, appetite, beast, body, breath, creature, x dead (-ly), desire, x [dis] contented, x fish, ghost,+ greedy, he, heart (-y), (hath, x jeopardy of) life (x in jeopardy), lust, man, me, mind, mortally, one, own, person, pleasure, (her-, him-, my-, thy-) self, them (your) -selves, +slay, soul, + tablet, they, thing, (x she) will, x would have it.[23] This word is, therefore, by its definition very much like the Greek word, *psuché*, which is describing the soul-life of men.	It is essential to be a truthful witness. It means that if I am to be the servant of God, I must speak to the issues that are there in fact. I must deal with the way things are in reality. I have never been so impressed with the idea of holding to truth so strongly before now in my life. What we see is that lives are at stake, and so help people to see things as they are. Get them to acknowledge the truth at least. "It is possible to acknowledge the truth but not love the truth. Whoever does not love the truth will go into deception."[24]	Prov. 14:5.

---

[23] James Strong, S.T.D., LL.D., *The New Strong's Complete Dictionary of Bible Words*, introduction by John R Kohlenberger, III, (Thomas Nelson Publishers:Atlanta, London,Vancouver, 1996)p. 456.

[24] Arthur J Stacer, January 2003, Arlington, TX Inner-City Evangelism mission trip.

Scripture	Observation	Applications	Cross-Ref
	This is speaking of the natural life (soul-life) that is being saved. A treacherous witness is one that betrays the trust of another.		
26 In the fear[3374] of the Lord there is strong confidence, and his children[1121] will have refuge.	This is the effect, or fruit of a life that turns from evil and does God's will, gaining a knowledge of the Holy One and a clear conscience.	Trust in His faithfulness and find stability amidst instability. Find in Him your refuge and you will have strong confidence.	Isaiah 33:6
27 The fear of the Lord is a fountain of life, that one may avoid [25] the snares of death.	Note the similarity between this verse, and Proverbs 13:14. In that verse it is the teaching of the wise that is a fountain of life that one may turn aside from the snares of death. So then one must have both the fear of the Lord, and the teaching of the wise. They come from the same fountain and they yield the same result. Also it is interesting to note how it speaks of the snares of death. There is not just one snare, but multiple snares. Each individual temptation to sin is a snare of death.	The fear of the Lord combined with the teachings of the wise, these will be a fountain of life. Do not forget the fear of the Lord, and pay attention to the teachings of the wise. Pay attention to the Word of God.	Prov. 8:13
28 In a multitude of people is a king's glory, but in the dearth of people[26] is a prince's ruin.	This suggests that the crown of a prince is the people over which he rules. A scarcity of people makes his crown insignificant and is the ruin of his kingship.	Even the Apostle Paul called the churches to which he ministered his glory and crown. Our crowns in the kingdom of the Lord will be those people to whom we ministered.	Phil 4:1 1Thess 2:19

---

[25] סור *sûr turn aside* (R.D.Patterson, Ph.D. *Theological Wordbook of the Old Testament, Vol II*, (Moody Press:Chicago, 1981) p.620).
This is the same word used in Proverbs 13:14.
[26] כתר *keter* **crown** (*Theological Wordbook of the Old Testament, Vol I*,(Moody Press:Chicago, 1981) p 460.)

Scripture	Observation	Applications	Cross-Ref
29 He who is slow to anger has great understanding, but he who is quick-tempered exalts folly.	The slow to anger displays wisdom; the quick-tempered exalt folly.	No greater advice can be given on the subject than that of James 1:19. "But let everyone be quick to hear, slow to speak and slow to anger; for the anger of man does not achieve the righteousness of God."[12]	James 1:19, 20
30 A tranquil heart is life to the body, but passion[13] is rottenness to the bones.	This word translated passion in the original relates to jealousy in the bad sense. Not only is it unhealthy to the body, but James tells us that where bitter jealousy and selfish ambition exists, there is also disorder and every evil thing.	If you detect jealousy in your heart, quickly go to the Lord in prayer and humble yourself and speak the truth.	James 3:16
31 He who oppresses the poor reproaches his Maker, but he who is gracious to the needy honors Him.	The poor and needy are a special concern to the Lord.	The poor and needy should be a special concern to you just as it is to the Lord, who preached the gospel to them and healed their diseases.	Luke 4:17-20.
32 The wicked is thrust down by his wrongdoing, but the righteous has a refuge when he dies.	The wicked do not have a refuge when they die. They will be thrust down. But the righteous have a refuge when they die —it is the Lord Himself. He is our refuge in this life; He is our refuge in the life to come.	What a refuge we have! Practice seeking God as a refuge, and when you die, it will not be a strange thing to find God is still your refuge.	Ps 1:4-6.
33 Wisdom rests in the heart of one who has understanding, but in the bosom of fools it is made known.	Wisdom settles down in the heart of one who has understanding, and even in the heart of a fool wisdom is made known, but it does not settle down in the fool's heart.	When you encounter wisdom, immediately take it to heart and let it quietly reside within your thoughts. Embrace it with all your zeal and act upon it in the opportune time.	Prov. 2:10.

---

[27] James 1:19, 20.

[28] קִנְאָה qin'â **ardor of jealousy, zeal, anger** This noun, modelled after the Qal infinitive form, describes the state wherein the subject is dominated by קָנָא--either positive or

149

Scripture	Observation	Applications	Cross-Ref
34 Righteousness exalts a nation, but sin is a disgrace to any people.	Righteousness raises a nation to a place of distinction and honor, but sin lowers the nation to disgrace and dishonor.	Teach righteousness to the people of my nation. Be an example of righteousness to those who know me. Talk of the fear of the Lord. Speak about loving God with all your heart.	Rom. 1:18-32
35 The king's favor is toward a servant who acts wisely, but his anger is toward him who acts shamefully	No one in authority wants to put up with those who through foolishness act shamefully, however, they will readily recognize the person who acts with wisdom and reward them.	Always conduct your daily affairs with wisdom, for it is the Lord Jesus Christ, the King of kings, whom you are serving.	Col. 3:23, 24.

negative. The central meaning of our word, *qānā*, however, relates to "jealousy" especially in the marriage **relationship.** (Leonard J. Coppes,Th.D., *Theological Wordbook of the Old Testament, Vol I,* (Moody Press:Chicago, 1981) p 802.)

Chapter 15: Disposition and the Tongue

Scripture	Observation	Applications	Cross-Ref
1. A gentle answer turns away wrath, but a harsh word stirs up anger	*rak* —*tender, soft, delicate* — *when applied to speech it means "soft words"*[29] *ʾeṣeb* —*sorrow*, **labor**--" The root *ʾāṣab* relates to physical pain as well as to emotional sorrow.[30] Implied is that these are words that cause emotional sorrow.	There is an obvious connection between the manner of speech and human emotion.. Indeed the tone of ones speech communicates things beyond the meanings of the words themselves. For instance, ones attitude or state of mind or emotions is conveyed by the tone expressed. Or the consideration, which one has for the feelings of distress that ones address might potentially have if spoken in a certain way, reveals sensitivity or lack thereof. And some things are said with the intention to cause harm, or they are said with the opposite motive. For this reason, each one must teach their hearts about how to guard that which comes forth out of their mouths. For the tongue can do both harm or good beyond measure.	Judg 8:1—3 Prov 25:15 1Sam 25:9—38
2. The tongue of the wise makes knowledge acceptable, but the mouth of fools spouts folly	*yatab* —**be good, be well, be glad, be pleasing.**[31] The speech of a wise man makes knowledge sensible, and beautiful.	This verse gives one a motivation to be wise, or wise in heart, for such is able to take knowledge and make it useful, sensible	Prov 12:23

[29] **White, William,Ph.D.**, <u>Theological Wordbook Of The Old Testament, Vol II</u>, (Moody Press:Chicago, 1981) *p. 848.*

[30] **Allen, Ronald B.,Th.D.**, <u>Theological Wordbook Of The Old Testament, Vol II.</u>,(Moody Press:Chicago, 1981) *p. 687.*

[31] **Gilchrist, Paul R. Ph.D.**, <u>Theological Wordbook Of The Old Testament, Vol I,</u>,(Moody Press:Chicago, 1981)*p.375.*

Scripture	Observation	Applications	Cross-Ref
	The mouth of the fool blows hot air, and turns his so-called knowledge into unacceptable nonsense.	and beautiful to others and thus help mankind. Remember, the mouth manifests one's character and state of mind or emotions to those who hear that which comes forth. But if it brings forth useful, sensible and beautiful things, not only will people be helped, but God will be glorified.	Prov 15:28 Prov 13:16
3. The eyes of the Lord are in every place, watching the evil and the good.	The bad or evil that He observes could be people, things, or circumstances. The same is true for the good that He observes. He sees adversity, and kindness, trouble and those who help in times of trouble. He sees the people who cause hardship and commit evil and He sees the people who counter the evil done with good. Nothing escapes His notice for He sees every place which includes every locality on earth, and every condition of every heart and mind of every person alive.	**First**, meditate on this until it grips your soul how great God is. **Second**, cultivate in your own heart a healthy fear of the Lord that leads you to hate evil, turn away from evil, love God's word and keep His commandments, and increase in your knowledge of God personally and experientially. **Third**, realize that after this life you will have to give account to Him who has observed all that has transpired in your life.	2Chr 16:9 Job 31:4 Ps 139:1—5 Jer 16:17 Zech 4:10 Heb 4:13
4. A soothing tongue is a tree of life, but perversion in it crushes the spirit.	This is speaking of the kind of speech that heals in the inner man. Perversion in speech causes affliction, destruction or a crushing in the spirit. This means that a person could suffer in their conscience with guilt, or could suffer loss of fellowship with God, and loss of perception of God's presence and God's activity in their lives.	We tend not to think of other people's inward struggles that they face day by day just as we do. If we wish to know love in all its dimensions shouldn't we train ourselves to think of those difficulties others must have. Shouldn't we show due consideration and thoughtfulness toward others? Isn't this the essential thing about love?	Prov 12:18

Scripture	Observation	Applications	Cross-Ref
		Shouldn't we come to sense their pain so that we can also speak to them in a soothing way, in a healing way, to help them in their conscience, to help them in their fellowship with the Lord? We must show consideration.	
5. A fool rejects his father's discipline, but he who regards[32] reproof is prudent.	Even though it is one's earthly father, there is a reminder in Prov 1:7 that fools despise instruction. Part of gaining wisdom is to pay attention to reproof, and the person who pays attention to it is considered both careful and wise. This also suggests that the fear of the Lord is a significant factor in one's motivation to listen to reproof.	Usually, it is not easy to listen to a rebuke. If it is based on truth due to the evidence, it can be quite traumatic indeed. It is at these moments when two things come into view: 1) Do you fear God? If the answer to this question is positive, you should quietly listen to what is being said. 2)Do you love the truth? Even if it turns out that a person's conclusion in all its particulars is not correct, still there may be a kernel of truth in the rebuke which you need to hear and apply to your life.	Prov 13:18
6. Much wealth is in the house of the righteous, but trouble is in the income of the wicked.	Since it is abundantly clear that not all righteous men and women are rich in money or material possessions, in this passage it must be speaking figuratively.	The acquisition of things and money is not evil. Here the verse is focusing on the righteous and the wicked. Obviously, the righteous would acquire things in a different way because they are not wicked. The strength and treasure of the righteous will stem from the	Luke 12:21

---

[32] *shamar —I keep, guard, observe, give heed.* In this usage, "it is used of a man's attitude of paying attention to, or reverence for, God or others." (**Hartley, John E., Ph.D.,** Theological Wordbook of the Old Testament, Vol II,(Moody Press:Chicago, 1981) *p. 940.*)

Scripture	Observation	Applications	Cross-Ref
		character qualities established in the details of how they lived from day to day. In their income there is no trouble because they came by it honestly whether it was little, or in abundance.	
7. The lips of the wise spread knowledge, but the hearts of fools are not so.	This verse contrasts the lips of the wise against the hearts of fools. But how does one know what is in the heart of the fool? By what comes out from the lips. And what does the lips of the wise reveal but what is on their hearts? Thus it is obvious that the fool who may believe he has knowledge in his heart does not have knowledge but folly. Implied is that the fool spreads folly. Folly is knowledge that is against God, against the fear of God, promotes pride and arrogance and evil, and speaks with perversion against the truth.	One's mouth gives away what is in the heart. And a person cannot conceal it completely. Most people do not guard it, and thus it becomes obvious whether or not they are fools or wise.	Ps 14:1 Ps 53:1 Matt 12:34
8. The sacrifice of the wicked is an abomination to the Lord, but the prayer of the upright is His delight.	*zebaḥ —sacrifice* Generic noun often linked with offerings (Ps 40:6 [**H7**]) or burnt offerings (1Sam 6:5; Ex 10:25).[33] This verse contrasts the burnt offerings of the wicked against the prayers of the upright. The burnt offerings are called an abomination and the prayers are His delight.	It is not the outward religious acts which please God, no matter what the sacrifice entails, but it is one's heart that God examines.	Gen 4:4—5.

---

[33] **Wolf, Herbert, Ph.D.**, <u>Theological Wordbook of the Old Testament</u>, Vol I, (Moody Press:Chicago, 1981) *p. 233*

Scripture	Observation	Applications	Cross-Ref
	Usually prayers of the upright are accompanied with humility, contrition, faith and intercession. These are not the things which accompany the actions of the wicked even when they try to practice religion, it is as though they believe it is their own works that will earn them favor with God.		
9. The way of the wicked is an abomination to the Lord, but He loves him who pursues righteousness.	*Pursue* —to strive to gain; seek to attain or accomplish (an end, object, purpose, etc.). *way* —*a metaphor* meaning the actions or behavior of men. In this verse, it is clear that the one action or behavior which is not to be seen with the wicked man or woman is the action of striving to gain righteousness, or seeking to attain righteousness or seeking to accomplish righteousness. Because He loves righteousness and hates lawlessness (Heb 1:9) how much more would He love those who pursue righteousness.	Pursue righteousness, but not a righteousness of your own, no, but a righteousness derived from God on the basis of faith in Christ. (Philippians 3:9)	Prov 21:21 1Tim 6:11 Prov 11:19
10. Stern discipline is for him who forsakes the way; he who hates reproof will die.	The "way" is a metaphor in this verse which refers to the path of righteousness, or righteous living. This verse is saying that for those who forsake the path of righteousness, there is very severe correction, and those who hate the inevitable reproof will die.	Do not forsake the way of righteousness. But if you do, accept the very serious correction that will come to you and repent.	Prov 12:1

Scripture	Observation	Applications	Cross-Ref
11. Sheol and Abaddon lie open before the Lord, How much more the hearts of men!	Since the Lord sees and knows the thoughts of those in the place of the dead, how much more does He know the thoughts, emotions and actions of those in the place of the living?	Isn't this a strong case for the fear of the Lord? How many times have we decided to sin because we erroneously thought that no one could see us? But if we remember that God sees everything even in our hearts then shouldn't that knowledge affect the things upon which we let our minds dwell, and the actions we take? Shouldn't it cause us to turn away from evil?	Lk 16:19—31 Heb 4:13
12. A scoffer does not love one who reproves him, He will not go to the wise.	It is clear that one of the tasks allotted to the wise is to reprove the scoffer. However, Prov 9:7 reminds us what will happen if one reproves the scoffer: "He who corrects a scoffer gets dishonor for himself,." And again, "Do not reprove a scoffer, lest he hate you, ..." (Prov 9:8) All this implies that a scoffer finds righteousness repulsive and considers the fear of God as worthless. A Christian can become a scoffer. And also, the phrase "the wise" is not a synonym for believer. In other words, a believer in the Lord can be quite foolish in their manner of life and disposition of heart.	There are two types of wisdom. 1. that which is of the world. 2. that which is from above. The "wise" in this verse is a reference to one whose wisdom comes from above, and excludes that one whose wisdom is of the earth. The former is spiritual, the latter is natural. Do not be afraid to seek the wisdom from above. Do not be afraid of a rebuke or of reproof. Associate with the wise and you will find life-giving reproof; as to the reproofs you have received from the wise, they are your life. (See Proverbs 15:31) The scoffer holds that which is spiritual in contempt.	Prov 13:1

Scripture	Observation	Applications	Cross-Ref
13. A joyful heart makes a cheerful face, But when the heart is sad, the spirit is broken.	This suggests that the root cause of a broken(or wounded) spirit is a wounded heart. The translation here uses the phrase: "the spirit is broken." One whose spirit is broken is marked by a loss of motivation, a lack of hope, a loss of purpose, a feeling of alienation, a confusion as to what is right. This person would more likely than not enter into a depression that practically disables him or her so that it becomes difficult to carry on with the daily tasks. The original language means a wounded heart. A person wounded in his or her emotions, thoughts or will, suffers also from a wounded spirit. Often the remedy must begin with an attempt to minister to the wounded spirit first.	God does not despise a broken spirit. Neither should we. If someone comes to you with a broken spirit you must help that person. You might have to stop what you are doing, And the person may call at a time inconvenient for you, say 11:30 at night. But do not brush it aside. Make yourself available to minister to that person's spirit. Often, a reminder of God's presence and working in his or her life will help to revive his or her faith. This is the goal then, to revive the faith of the one who is depressed, so as to restore his or her hope and purpose and to clarify the facts and reaffirm what is right. In this way, he or she can recover from the wound and will know the grace of God-- the presence and activity of God influencing the mind, will and emotions producing in one's life gratitude.	Prov 12:25
14. The mind of the intelligent seeks knowledge, but the mouth of fools feeds on folly.	The contrast in this verse is between a seeking mind of one who has insight versus the feeding mouth of a fool, hungry for folly. This verse could be translated: the mind of him who has insight seeks knowledge.	This kind of knowledge is sought by: 1.*observation* and *awareness* of that which is all around. 2. *contemplation* or thoughtful meditation. 3. and *drawing near to God* in prayer and studying His Word.	Prov 2:1-5

Scripture	Observation	Applications	Cross-Ref
	This speaks of a person who has a grasp of things such that he or she is able to distinguish between good and evil. Such a one is marked by a pursuit of knowledge.	The heart of a man or woman who has insight seeks for the knowledge of God. This is indicating the desire of the one with understanding is just the opposite of the fool who has an appetite for folly. This verse is pointing to what a person takes into themselves. A fool consumes foolishness but a wise man seeks the knowledge that enables him to possess moral cognition and contemplative insight into the unseen things of God.	
15. All the days of the afflicted[34] are bad, But a cheerful heart has a continual feast.	When a person is depressed either in his or her mind or because of his or her circumstances, every day seems not to be good in any manner or to any degree. But when a person has a cheerful (or good) heart, each day seems to be a continual feast. Why is it that the days of the depressed are bad? It is speaking from the perspective of the depressed one. His or her mind is depressed because their perspective, their way of seeing it, is focused on themselves and on their plight.	Be good-hearted and your days will go better. Observe those who think that every day is not good in any manner or to any degree and help them, for they are depressed. You must help them shift their focus from self to the Lord. From the bad circumstances to the sovereign purposes of the Lord.	Rom 8:28

---

[34] 6041 עָנִי aw-nee' from 6031; depressed, in mind or circumstances (practically the same as 6035, although the margin constantly disputes this, making 6035 subjective and 6041 objective):--afflicted, humble, lowly, needy, poor. see HEBREW for 06031 see HEBREW for 06035 see HEBREW for 06035 see HEBREW for 06041 (Strong's Dictionary of Hebrew Words)

Scripture	Observation	Applications	Cross-Ref
	But the one with the good heart sees the same afflictions in a different way. They will look at it from the perspective that there is an all loving and wise God who knows all things and He has a purpose for all things in our lives. This is why a person who continually trusts in the lovingkindness of the Lord sees even the difficult things as evidence of His love.		
16. Better is a little with the fear of the Lord, than great treasure and turmoil with it.	The Fear of the Lord is more excellent than riches. Even if one has little of this world's goods but has the fear of the Lord, they are better off than those who have the material things of this world in abundance, and the turmoil which comes with it, but do not have the fear of the Lord.	Fear the Lord no matter what you have in this world. It will go better for you because the fear of the Lord will bring peace into your life even if you are poor.	Ps 37:16
17. Better is a dish of vegetables where love is, than a fattened ox and hatred with it.	Love makes all the difference in life. It does not matter when there is love if all you can afford to eat is vegetables. On the other hand, if you are well to do and have steaks all the time, but there is hatred in your hearts towards the ones with whom you share your feast, what value is this? A carnal man may choose the beef to gratify his appetite and just be concerned with himself and his desires with little regard for the others, but this is great emptiness. A man should choose the things that endure to eternity. A wise person sees the people as more important than the event no matter how large or small the event may be.	"Do not work for the food that perishes, but for the food that endures to eternal life, which the Son of Man shall give to you. For on him the Father, even God, has set his seal." Jn 6:27	Isa 55:2

Scripture	Observation	Applications	Cross-Ref
18 A hot-tempered man stirs up strife, but the slow to anger pacifies contention.	This is the second verse in this chapter that tells how strife is stirred up. The first verse of this chapter tells us that harsh words stir up strife. This verse tells us that it is a hot-tempered man that does it. It is no wonder, for the hot-tempered man surely will speak harsh words. Harsh words are irritating and unpleasant to one's emotions. One who is hot-tempered is emotional, not rational.	You cannot allow yourself to be controlled by the flesh, namely, emotions run amuck . You must be controlled by the Spirit, therefore, yield to the Spirit. As a Christian, I must acknowledge that the scriptures call outbursts of anger works of the flesh in contrast to the fruit of the Spirit.	Jas 1:19
19 The way of a **sluggard** is as a hedge of thorns, but the path of the **upright** is a highway.	This verse speaks of the effect of the manner and habits of a lazy indolent person as compared to the effect of a person whose manner and habits are pleasing to God. What is characteristic of a sluggard is a strong disinclination to exert oneself, or a great dislike for work such that they become lazy or idle and waste time by their idleness. Thus they habitually do nothing. This is in contrast to the upright by implication, make the most of their time, and do those things that are pleasing to God. The hedge of thorns implies an obstacle, and the highway implies no obstacles but a more efficient travel through life.	In walking upright, in every aspect of my life, I must not be lazy. To overcome one's dislike for exerting oneself, it is necessary to change one's point of view and see that diligence is an attitude and disposition which pleases God and Idleness does not please Him. If I am to be useful to Him, I cannot be lazy, especially in the work of God. Secondly, realize that laziness is an attitude of those who do wickedness. If I am to be upright I cannot be lazy. Negligence is no longer an option. Thus it is wise to consider that laziness is in fact foolishness. One should not allow themselves to deviate from the path of the upright, but be thorough, paying close attention	Eph 5:15—17

Scripture	Observation	Applications	Cross-Ref
		to the details, so as to make the most of one's time to be useful both to God and men, as aservant should be during this short life span upon the earth.	
20 A wise son makes a father glad, but a foolish man despises his mother.	It seems that most children want their father's approval, and in this case, it is a wise-hearted child who wins the father's delight. But it is quite a different matter with a foolish man, whose attitude of contempt towards his mother is seen here. This verse shifts from its focus on the feelings of the parent to the feelings of the foolish man. And those feelings are ones of disrespect.	Perhaps it is the mother who is most hurt by the foolishness of a son, or a daughter. When proverbs speak of a wise son, it most certainly means a son who fears the Lord. (Prov 1:7) But when it speaks of a foolish son it without doubt refers to a son who hates knowledge, righteousness, and the things of God thus he refuses the instruction of a mother.	Prov 29:3
21. Folly is a joy to one who lacks sense, but a man of understanding follows an upright course.	This kind of joy attributed to the man lacking sense will come to an end.[35] But the righteous will know everlasting joy because they followed an upright course.	Both the future's potentiality and the past's finality are affected by the choices made in the present. The enormous importance of making the most of our time to work God's will is revealed by this understanding. The end will be everlasting joy.	Isa 32:17; 51:1 James 3:18 2Jn 4 3Jn 4

---

[35] Bruce K. Waltke wrote, "The occasions for joy are manifold: against God, apart from God, and with God.

"The heathen rejoice when they triumph over Israel (Jud 16:23) and the fool finds joy in his folly (Prov 15:21). But such joy must end, for the righteous will find everlasting joy (Isa 51:11)"[**Waltke, Bruce K.,Th.D., Ph.D.,**Theological Wordbook of the Old Testament, *Vol II,*(*Moody Bible Institute:Chicago, 1980*)*p. 879*].

Scripture	Observation	Applications	Cross-Ref
22. Without counsel [36] plans fail, but with many advisors they succeed.	This seems to be speaking of a group of people assembled to discuss confidential matters and determine the best course. Plans which are determined by such counsel tend to succeed. But an unwillingness to seek such confidence among friends may doom one's plans to failure.	Two things immediately surface: 1) transparency 2) trust. In order to bring something confidential to a group of trusted advisors, I must be willing to be transparent. In order to be transparent, I must trust the people whose counsel I seek. A third issue comes forward: that of teachability. If my counselors are wise-hearted people, I must listen to what they say, and alter my plans accordingly.	Prov 11:14; Prov 20:18
23. A man has joy in an apt answer, and how delightful is a timely word!	When a man is able to give an answer to a given issue which is exactly correct and especially suitable to the purpose, and/or the person, and/or the occasion, according to the need of the moment, then he finds joy in such an answer. Perhaps the joy stems from the realization of the value of the answer, and its positive effect on the person, or occasion.	Only God can impart such an ability to a man. It requires wisdom to give such an answer, and this is the point of the Proverbs of Solomon, to gain understanding, to learn wisdom, to grasp what is right, and to be able to impart it to those around them. But reading and studying Proverbs alone will not give a man this ability. Along with the study and meditation upon these sayings, there must be prayer to the One who gave it to Solomon.	Eph 4:29 James 1:5

---

[36] סוֹד (*sôd*) **counsel, council, assembly**. (RSV occasionally reads "gatherings", "company") The primary meaning of the word is "confidential speech" (cf. Arabic *sā' wada* "speak secretly") hence, "counsel" The emphasis on confidentiality marks a distinction between this word and the more general *ēṣâ* (q.v.) "advice", "counsel".

The word stresses that intelligent counsel can be a key to good success (Prov 15:22). It is extended to indicate a circle of trusted intimates who gave their advice (Ps 55:14 [H 15]; 83:3 [H 4]). Hopefully, such friends will never stand against a man (Job 19:19) or reveal confidences (Prov 11:13; 30:19; 25:9). [**R.D. Patterson, Ph.D.**, Theological Wordbook of the Old Testament, *Vol II*, (Moody Press:Chicago, 1981) *p 619*].

Scripture	Observation	Applications	Cross-Ref
		Seek His face and He will enlighten your understanding if you seek Him with all your heart.	
24. The path of life leads upward for the wise, that he may keep away from Sheol below.	Paul instructs the Christians to seek the things above, and set their minds on the things above. This means that it is spiritual things that we should seek and spiritual things which should occupy our thoughts or we will shorten our lives by fleshly thinking which leads to living wickedly.	Faith in Christ alone will deliver a man completely from the grave. Because in Christ death has been abolished (2Tim 1:10) and life and immortality has been brought to light through the gospel. Even so, the Christian is instructed in the NT to set his or her mind on spiritual things (the things above) so as to be delivered from the fleshly living that inevitably results from setting ones mind on the things that are fleshly or worldly..	Colossians 3:1, 2 Rom 8:13
25. The Lord will tear down the house of the proud, but He will establish the boundary of the widow.	The Lord is in opposition to the arrogance of men but is a defender of the widow.

First, on the one hand, with regard to the proud, the scriptures are clear: God opposes them (James 4:6; 1Peter 5:5). And the prospect of being destroyed by the Lord is revealed here in this verse.

But on the other hand we see His inclination to be a defender of the widow. (Deut 10:18;Ps 68:5;Ps 146:9;Jer 22:3;Jas 1:27) | What is the Lord like? This verse shows that He destroys, and He defends. But what does He destroy? The house (family) of the proud. Therefore, do not become proud. If you are already proud then humble yourself immediately. For God is opposed to you. We also learn that God cares about people who are widows, orphans or strangers (immigrants). Shouldn't we also care for them and defend them? The answer is obviously, "yes." | Prov 29:23; Prov 23:10,11 |

Scripture	Observation	Applications	Cross-Ref
26. Evil plans are an abomination to the Lord, but pleasant words are pure.	Evil plans (thoughts) come from hearts filled with evil intent. But the type of words called pleasant are pure because they come from hearts whose intention is pure. The implication is that the LORD loves the purity of the heart of the one who is speaking pleasant words.	What is a pure heart as revealed in the scripture? Philippians 1:15—18 illustrates both a pure attitude from some people toward another man, and an impure state of mind toward the same man from different persons. On the one hand, a person is proclaiming Christ out of love. This is why it is pure. On the other hand, a person was doing the same thing, but out of envy and rivalry. Their intent was to cause harm to the imprisoned Apostle Paul. What they were doing was evil because they were filled with envy and strife. They wanted to inflict harm on someone else, and that is evil. But Paul showed a good heart about it and gave thanks to God that Christ was being proclaimed	Matthew 5:8. **Philippians 1:15—18.**
27. He who profits illicitly troubles his own house, But he who hates bribes will live.	He who takes a bribe is willing to corrupt his life for material gain. This corruption not only affects his own soul, but all his relationships become corrupted.	There is a saying that goes like this: "Every man has his price." This is true for every man who is willing to be seduced by money and forfeit good character. Yes, a bribe corrupts the conduct and the character of the one receiving it. What a tragic exchange, the loss of something priceless for something that perishes.	1Timothy 6:10

Scripture	Observation	Applications	Cross-Ref
		Never make such an exchange. It will ruin your life, family, reputation, and fruitfulness especially in the spiritual realm.	
28. The heart of the righteous ponders how to answer, but the mouth of the wicked pours out evil things.	The righteous guard their hearts and the hearts by not just pouring out evil things.	Be quick to hear, slow to speak.	James 1:19
29. The Lord is far from the wicked, but He hears the prayer of the righteous.	Clearly there is communion between the just and the Lord, but no such communion exists between the wicked and the Lord. Communion is one of the functions of the human spirit. It is seen in prayer, meditation, praise, and worship. It is the place wherein one interacts with the living God. Communion with the Lord is possible for those who have been made alive to God in Christ Jesus. If one is living righteously, that one will have sweet communion with the Lord.	"Submit therefore to God. Resist the devil and he will flee from you. Draw near to God, and He will draw near to you. Cleanse your hands you sinners, purify your hearts you double-minded." (James 4:7,8)	Hebrews 5:7
30. Bright eyes gladden the heart; good news puts fat on the bones.	More likely than not, this is speaking figuratively about the effect on our mind, will and emotions that light, or spiritual truth, has as it is perceived and understood by a person. Its light brightens the soul.	Knowing this effect, how important is it that our souls should be brightened by the light that God gives through His Word? And if one is thus brightened, shouldn't that one also share that light with others as well?	Ps 119:130, 135
31. He whose ear listens to the life-giving reproof will dwell among the wise.	The companion of wise men will inevitably be reproved, and if he listens to the reproof it will give him life.	Be a companion of wise men. Listening to reproof is a mark of one who fears the LORD.	Prov 13:20

Scripture	Observation	Applications	Cross-Ref
32. He who neglects discipline despises himself, but he who listens to reproof acquires understanding.	If a person listens to reproof he demonstrates that he has a healthy view of himself, and will acquire understanding.	Acquiring understanding is also a mark of the fear of the LORD, and this kind of gain comes from listening to reproof.	Job 28:28
33. The fear of the Lord is the instruction for wisdom, and before honor comes humility.	The fear of the LORD comes before wisdom. Humility comes before honor. There must be humility in the fear of the LORD just as there is honor in wisdom.	"Humble yourselves in the presence of the LORD, and He will exalt you." (James 4:10).	Isaiah 66:2

Printed in the United States
by Baker & Taylor Publisher Services